Inspired* by music

shoehorn

First published in the UK in 2009 by
Shoehorn Arts & Culture Books, an imprint of
Shoehorn Publishing, which is a division of
Shoehorn Media Ltd, 4 Great Marlborough Street, London W1F 7HH, UK
www.shoehornbooks.com
www.shoehorn.biz

A CIP catalogue record for this book is available from the British Library.
ISBN: 9781907149016

Printed in the UK by Butler Tanner and Dennis.

Inspired* by music

Personal reflections of how music changed our lives...

The Prince's Trust would especially like to thank the young people who have shared their stories

I am delighted to be able to introduce this songbook of inspirational music on behalf of my Trust.

It seems to me that music is a fascinating phenomenon because, on the one hand, it is a truly universal language that knows no barriers of origin, creed or circumstance, and therefore has the capacity to engage us all. On the other, its expression and enjoyment is entirely personal, and so often the memory of a particular piece of music is bound up with an event in our lives.

I am most grateful to each of the contributors to this songbook for telling us about a particular time in which one piece of music has struck them. I hope their choice will encourage others - either through the music itself or by the story behind it.

To the young people whom my Trust has been able to help in some way, and whose selections appear in this songbook, Catherine Allen, Jamie Turner, Julien Hughes-John, and Lisa Daly, I would like to express my particular thanks.

However difficult or empty anyone's life may seem at times, music can still provide a reminder of hope…

I am delighted to say that the proceeds of this songbook will go entirely to my Trust and will thus enable it to reach and help more young people in the future. I do hope that, through the music, you too may find some degree of inspiration.

Introduction by Phil Collins

Music: I've lived and worked with it all my life; in fact it's *been* my life. Yet it still has the power to surprise, amaze, captivate and enthral me. Where does it come from? What makes it such a powerful and emotional force? How would we survive without it?

Now, more than ever before, music surrounds us. It really is the soundtrack to our lives. When we listen alone, on a car stereo or through our iPod headphones, it cocoons us with its comforting familiarity: it is personal, intimate, it connects with the soul. But music also has the power to bring people together, to inspire and motivate them. From pipers and drums leading troops into battle to the chants of football fans on the grandstand, music is a powerful force.

It is impossible to imagine a public occasion – celebration or commemoration – without music. From the memorable, embarrassing, first dance at a family wedding to the sombre, sobering hymn singing at a funeral, music binds us.

Music also inspires us through the less public, more personal moments in our lives. When I hear certain songs they instantly transport me back in time and allow me to remember moments that otherwise might lay dormant.

I think it is particularly appropriate that a book about inspiration should be in aid of youth charity The Prince's Trust. I am proud to have been the first ambassador for The Trust in 1983 and was delighted to perform in fundraising concerts way back in 1982.

This charity does amazing work with disadvantaged and disenfranchised young people who feel their lives have no direction. The Prince's Trust provides a spark of inspiration, backed with practical support, to help them turn their lives around. Proceeds from the sale of this book will help The Trust continue its vital work, changing more young lives.

There are many people to thank for bringing this special publication to life – not least those people whose personal stories unfold throughout its pages. They have all given their time for free. I'm also delighted to contribute to this project in some small way, by writing this introduction. I'm especially grateful to The Trust for inviting me to do so and not that gorilla…

"I thought it had a real passion in it...

To me it was an attack on racism and prejudice of all kinds."

You've got to be Carefully Taught
Rodgers and Hammerstein

You've got to be Carefully Taught is from that great musical, *South Pacific*, by Rodgers and Hammerstein. I remember going to the show with my elementary school. It was a crucial time in our country's history when the racial tension in the south was raging and the play was a direct reference to it. The musical made such an impression on me at a very young age, especially this song. I thought it had a real passion in it and a relevance to the times we were living in with segregation as a main issue. To me it was an attack on racism and prejudice of all kinds. It had a real value and for something like that to appear in a romantic musical gave it additional power, since it wasn't expected. I liked it so much then and always have.

You've got to be Carefully Taught

Lyric by Oscar Hammerstein II, music by Richard Rodgers

You've got to be taught to hate and fear.
You've got to be taught from year to year.
It's got to be drummed in your dear little ear.
You've got to be carefully taught.

You've got to be taught to be afraid
Of people whose eyes are oddly made,
And people whose skin is a diff'rent shade,
You've got to be carefully taught.

You've got to be taught before it's too late,
Before you are six or seven or eight,
To hate all the people your relatives hate,
You've got to be carefully taught!
You've got to be carefully taught!

Al Pacino is one of the greatest actors of our time. Best known for his roles as Michael Corleone in *The Godfather* Trilogy and Tony Montana in *Scarface*, Al was born in Harlem, Manhattan. In his first film role, in 1969's *Me, Natalie*, he played a junkie. It was his ability to convincingly portray addiction that started his career. To date Al has received eight Oscar nominations, winning countless awards, appearing in 30 feature films and most importantly, winning the respect of his peers. In the past he has supported a number of charities including AIDS Healthcare Foundation, Amnesty International and Make Poverty History.

"Listening to this song over and over, I made up my mind to go for it and stick with it..."

I'd do Anything for Love (But I Won't do That)
Meatloaf

It was *I'd do Anything for Love* sung by Meatloaf that gave me the courage as a young soldier to attempt selection for 21 SAS.

I remember being not only scared of failing, but also scared of the pain that would inevitably lie ahead. But I have since learned that such fear is there to sharpen us and is the necessary price of achievement.

Listening to this song over and over, I made up my mind to go for it and stick with it – whatever the costs, the discomfort or the sacrifice. In order to pass, I vowed I would never quit. I would throw myself into it, heart, body, mind and soul and not count the cost.

The SAS often speaks of "many being called but few being chosen". The truth is that people pass or fail themselves by their attitude. Are they quitters when times get tough, or are they stickers? Are they willing to pay the price?

Looking back, it was that decision to never give up, regardless, that ultimately led to my passing Special Forces selection and from that point almost every worthwhile door in my life opened up.

My time with 21 SAS gave me the confidence to pursue my climbing ambitions afterwards. It gave me the self-belief that I could achieve some special things in my life and it gave me the realisation that we need each other and it is OK to depend on people sometimes. Together we are always stronger.

All this came from a willingness to take a risk. But the man who risks nothing gains nothing.

Enthusiasm and determination count for so much more than skills, brains or qualifications… and all this expressed itself to me through Meatloaf's song!

Bear Grylls is a British adventurer, television presenter and writer who entered the record books in 1997 as the youngest Briton to climb Ama Dablam in the Himalayas.

In 1998, aged 23, Grylls became the youngest Briton to summit Mount Everest, 18 months after breaking his back in a freefall accident.

Bear has led many expeditions around the world including crossing the Arctic Ocean in an open RIB in aid of The Prince's Trust, a feat for which he was awarded an honorary commission in the Royal Navy.

Bear has been a supporter of The Trust ever since and today hosts one of the highest rating adventure TV shows on earth: *Born Survivor*, reaching a global audience of 1.2 billion. This features Bear being dropped into some of the most hostile terrains on earth and showing how to stay alive!

I'd do Anything for Love (But I Won't do That)
Words and music by Jim Steinman

And I would do anything for love.
I'd run right into hell and back.
I would do anything for love.
I'll never lie to you and that's a fact.
But I'll never forget the way you feel right now, oh no, no way.
And I would do anything for love, but I won't do that.
No, I won't do that.

Some days it don't come easy,
Some days it don't come hard.
Some days it don't come at all
And these are the days that never end.
Some nights you're breathing fire,
some nights you're carved in ice.
Some nights are like nothing I've ever seen before or will again.
Maybe I'm crazy,
But it's crazy and it's true.
I know you can save me.
No one else can save me now but you.
As long as the planets are turning,
As long as the stars are burning,
As long as your dreams are coming true,
You better believe it

That I would do anything for love.
Oh, I would do anything for love.
Oh, I would do anything for love,
But I won't do that.
No, I won't do that.
I would do anything for love,
Anything you've been dreaming of,
But I just won't do that.
I would do anything for love, anything you've been dreaming of,
But I just won't do...

Some days I pray for silence,
Some days I pray for soul.
Some days I just pray

To the god of sex and drums and rock 'n' roll.
Maybe I'm lonely,
And that's all I'm qualified to be.
There's just one and only,
The one and only promise I can keep.
As long as the wheels are turning,
As long as the fires are burning,
As long as your prayers are coming true,
You better believe it

That I would do anything for love
And you know it's true and that's a fact.
I would do anything for love,
And there'll never be no turning back.
But I'll never do it better than I do it with you.
So long, so long.
And I would do anything for love.
Oh, I would do anything for love.
I would do anything for love,
But I won't do that, no, no, no, I won't do that.

(Will you raise me up, will you help me down?
Will you get me right out of the godforsaken town?
Will you make it a little less cold?)
I can do that, oh no, I can do that.
(Will you cater to ev'ry fantasy I got?
Will you hose me down with holy water
If I get too hot?
Will you take me places I've never gone?)
I can do that, oh no, I can do that
(I know the territory. I've been around.
It'll all turn to dust and we'll all fall down.
Sooner or later you'll be screwing around.)
I won't do that.
No, I won't do that.
Anything for love, but I won't do that.

"…songs that trigger memories make you work that little bit harder to achieve your goal."

Chariots of Fire
Vangelis

As a kid growing up this was always powerful music and certainly always good to listen to through periods when I needed motivation or needed to start concentrating for a big event. I started training seriously when I was 15, with an ambition to go to the Olympic Games.

There are songs that remind me of particular occasions, like achieving my first gold at the Sydney Olympics in 2000, but it's *Chariots of Fire* that really inspires me.

When you're training hard, you need a bit of motivation to keep going and certainly music like this, music that trigger memories that make you work that little bit harder to achieve your goal, often help.

If things aren't going that well or you need an extra kick, this music helps at that moment in time but also helps you think about what's important, why you're doing something.

Chariots of Fire

Vangelis

This instrumental piece was the theme
music to the 1981 feature film of the
same name, based on the true story of
British athletes competing in the 1924 Olympics.
The composer Vangelis won an Academy Award
for best Original Music Score and the title theme
became a hit in its own right, topping the
US Billboard Chart in 1982.

Words and music by Evangelos Papathanassiou (Vangelis) © 1981.
Reproduced by permission of EMI Music Publishing Ltd., London W8 5SW

Ben Ainslie CBE is Britain's most successful Olympic sailor, gaining three gold medals and one silver. Not only is Ben a triple Olympic gold medalist but he is also a nine times World Champion and eight times European Champion.

Since the Beijing 2008 Olympics, Ben has received many awards and was most recently honoured with a CBE in Her Majesty The Queen's New Year Honours List. Ben also became the only sailor ever to be crowned ISAF World Sailor of the Year three times and British Yachtsman of the Year five times.

Ben's next aspiration is to win the America's Cup as skipper with Team Origin before setting his sights on the London 2012 Olympics and bringing back an historic fourth gold.

"It reminds me of a sense of reality, even humour and with it, a reason for hope."

How to Disappear Completely
Radiohead

I had gone to South Africa to make a BBC series called *To the Ends of the Earth* and on a weekend off I went with two friends to do a diving course in the stunning Sodwana Bay. Coming down with a cold and feeling nervous about making it back early in the morning, I selfishly pulled rank and suggested we break a cardinal rule by driving after dark.

I will always remember that *How to Disappear Completely* by Radiohead was playing. This haunting track was half-way through, the window was down and we were relaxing into the journey. That's when things started to go wrong. The front right tyre blew and we pulled up after 100 yards to fix it. It was 8pm, pitch dark and we were two hours from home. There was traffic on the highway, but the rule is you never stop, not even for other drivers who may be in trouble. We were on our own.

I tried to change the wheel but I'm no mechanic and I couldn't get the jack to fit. Theo and Denise called the South African equivalent of the AA, but our hopes for them arriving were slim. Although we said nothing to each other, we were all feeling tense and nervous. Stories of car jacking were fresh in our minds.

Out of the shadows of the bush we were suddenly aware of a group of six men moving towards us. It all happened so quickly. Theo calmly warned us not to look at them and do what they asked. They made us stand facing the car with our hands on our heads and were carrying what looked like weapons of some sort.

They frisked each of us for weapons and valuables and we cursed the fact that we'd paid for our diving course in cash – all we had in our wallets were bank cards.

They bundled us back into the car and I remember thinking that they wanted to shoot us in the car and then drive it off the road. Theo and Denise were in the back and I had to sit in the front passenger seat on the lap of one of men, with my back to the windscreen and my head down. I was terrified. It seemed surreal. The guy I was sat on started to frisk me again and it freaked me out him touching me and so I looked directly at him and said, "What are you doing? What do you want? Just take our belongings and don't hurt us." Denise was trying to reason with them but Theo, who owned the car and lived in Johannesburg, told her to shut up. He became our spokesperson.

They drove the car off the road and into the bush. As we bumped over the sandy path further into the blackness, my bum hit the stereo and that Radiohead track we had been listening to burst on. The car stopped and we were bundled out and told to kneel with our hands on our heads. I tried to stand, as I knew I was about to be sick but they ordered us to kneel down and they took off our shoes. We were in the execution position with a duvet over our heads to silence the shots, beneath an underpass with HGVs thundering past above – the perfect cover for gunshots. They'd driven off-road to rob and shoot us, fix the car and drive off unobserved. "This is it!" I thought.

We waited but nothing happened. Then they tossed the duvet off us and demanded to know who owned the phones and cards they had found and why we had no cash or drugs. As a South African, Theo was doing most of the talking. South Africans are more expendable than Brits in the eyes of criminals – so when he started explaining that Denise and I were not South African, but were English actors, he was selflessly helping us gain a high status in our captors' eyes, although at the time I was fearful it made us a more precious commodity for a ransom.

By now the men had changed the flat. They intended to drive somewhere and use our cards in a machine. Unaware of the danger I was in and disorientated by the nausea and cramp that was still cripplingly uncomfortable, I again tried to stand. To them this was clearly a sign of panic or evasion. They ordered me to stand up and get into the boot of the car. With the lid shut I could hear the others pleading. I don't remember panicking but I must have shouted and the boot lid opened. I started to reason that this was not a good idea but they shut the boot again.

What are they doing to the others? Are they going to kill them while I'm trapped in here? I heard Den saying "Please don't kill him." Christ they're going to kill me in the boot! The lid opened and I found myself calmly lying that I was claustrophobic and that while I had enough air to breath, I could panic and die and be a problem for them. "Dead body in a boot, problem, not good!" The lid slammed shut again. A lot of arguing. It opened again and they told me to get out.

They took me up a small hill away from the others. I fell over and cut my head on the ground. Once again they made me kneel and tied my hands behind my back with laces from the trainers they'd removed earlier. I heard "We are not going to hurt you but make one mistake and we will kill you. Lie on the ground." I could hear the others being brought up and Den talking calmly about being cold and needing to be tied to me for warmth. Theo had gone silent and I feared the worst but thankfully he was brought to the same spot and tied up. The car sounded like it was leaving and that we were being guarded by only a couple of the gang.

I was on my side with my eyes closed and my ear to the ground. I was frozen in stillness and cold. I could feel the blood on my face and hear the insects scratching around in the dark. I thought of home and how, despite being near other people, we all die utterly alone. I started a breathing meditation to recover calm, conserve energy and remain alert.

At times it seemed that the men had gone, then they would come back. This happened a few times…and then nothing. We told each other that they were gone and began to untie ourselves. We could hardly walk at first, but eventually stumbled up the embankment and on to the road.

Cars and lorries passed and we tried to stop them but by now it was around 11pm – cars and lorries stop for no-one.

After 15 minutes of losing hope we saw a sign and ran. It was a part open-air game shop, part curio shop, a co-operative run by women that served as a truck stop at night. They welcomed us and comforted us in our tears and explanations of what happened, clutching their faces in concern and clicking in anger that we had experienced this in their country. I wept as an African man's hand reached down to untie one of the remaining shoelaces on my wrist. I wrote as we waited for the police and production company, sipping an instant coffee and smoking a cigarette that were the best of my life.

I went back to the spot where it happened. In the daylight it seemed very small but it still belonged to that night and us. When I hear that Radiohead song, it doesn't so much bring back the terror and the horror but instead reminds me of a sense of reality, even humour and with it, a reason for hope that somehow I would survive a small event in a big country and escape to live a fuller life.

" This haunting track was half-way through, the window was down and we were relaxing into the journey. That's when things started to go wrong. "

How to Disappear Completely
Thom Yorke/Phillip Selway/Edward O'Brien/
Colin Greenwood/Jonathan Greenwood

That there
That's not me
I go
Where I please
I walk through walls
I float down the Liffey
I'm not here
This isn't happening
I'm not here
I'm not here

In a little while
I'll be gone
The moment's already passed
Yeah it's gone
And I'm not here
This isn't happening
I'm not here
I'm not here

Strobe lights and blown speakers
Fireworks and hurricanes
I'm not here
This isn't happening
I'm not here
I'm not here

Benedict Cumberbatch is one of the UK's leading young actors. To many he is best known for his acclaimed portrayal of Stephen Hawking in the BBC drama, *Hawking*, for which he was nominated as Best Actor at the 2005 British Academy Television Awards.

His numerous other television roles include *Stuart: A Life Backwards*, *Broken News*, *To the Ends of the Earth*, *Nathan Barley* and *Dunkirk*. In 2008 he starred in the tense BBC drama *The Last Enemy* and his most recent role is as Sherlock Holmes in the major forthcoming TV production, *Sherlock*.

In January 2006, he was nominated for an Olivier Award for 'Best Performance in a Supporting Role' when he played Tesman in *Hedder Gabler*. Other stage performances include George in Tennessee Williams' play *Period of Adjustment* and lead roles in *The City*, *Rhinoceros* and *The Arsonist* at The Royal Court Theatre in 2007/8.

His many film credits include *Atonement, The Other Boleyn Girl, Amazing Grace* and *Starter For Ten*.

> ❝ **There is absolutely nothing wrong with this song. It is perfect.** ❞

Things Have Changed
Bob Dylan

The fact that I find this song inspiring could indicate that I am not in very good shape, given that it contains some grim observations of how bad things can get. What is uplifting, apart from its general brilliance, is that it is thrilling to know that you are not alone in these matters. It's also, as his songs often are, amusing.

Any song containing the couplet "Feel like falling in love with the first woman I meet, putting her in a wheelbarrow and wheeling her down the street" is more than fine with me. There is absolutely nothing wrong with this song. It is perfect. It obviously appeals to my isolationist tendency, but at least it swings. The refrain is an anthem for people like myself, who should probably get out more.

Things Have Changed
Bob Dylan

A worried man with a worried mind
No one in front of me and nothing behind
There's a woman on my lap and she's drinking champagne
Got white skin, got assassin's eyes
I'm looking up into the sapphire tinted skies
I'm well dressed, waiting on the last train

Standing on the gallows with my head in a noose
Any minute now I'm expecting all hell to break loose

People are crazy and times are strange
I'm locked in tight, I'm out of range
I used to care, but things have changed

This place ain't doing me any good
I'm in the wrong town, I should be in Hollywood
Just for a second there I thought I saw something move
Gonna take dancing lessons do the jitterbug rag
Ain't no shortcuts, gonna dress in drag
Only a fool in here would think he's got anything to prove

Lot of water under the bridge, lot of other stuff too
Don't get up gentlemen, I'm only passing through

People are crazy and times are strange
I'm locked in tight, I'm out of range
I used to care, but things have changed

I've been walking forty miles of bad road
If the bible is right, the world will explode
I've been trying to get as far away from myself as I can
Some things are too hot to touch
The human mind can only stand so much
You can't win with a losing hand

Feel like falling in love with the first woman I meet
Putting her in a wheelbarrow and wheeling her down the street

People are crazy and times are strange
I'm locked in tight, I'm out of range
I used to care, but things have changed

I hurt easy, I just don't show it
You can hurt someone and not even know it
The next sixty seconds could be like an eternity
Gonna get low down, gonna fly high
All the truth in the world adds up to one big lie
I'm in love with a woman who don't even appeal to me

Mr Jinx and Miss Lucy, they jumped in the lake
I'm not that eager to make a mistake

People are crazy and times are strange
I'm locked in tight, I'm out of range
I used to care, but things have changed

Bill Nighy has been fortunate enough to play a widish range of parts. In recent years he has been required to be a zombie, a vampire and a squid. He has, it seems, reached that difficult age, where he can only portray men from other dimensions. He has also developed a line in sad, shallow, unreliable, rock idiots. He has mystifyingly never been selected for the more classical side of things, about which, he is quietly relieved as he is not entirely confident he could operate in those kind of trousers. When appearing in public, he likes to look his best.

"It is to be recommended to anyone contemplating a career in politics, or journalism, or indeed as any other kind of human being."

The Character of a Happy Life
Sir Henry Wotton

We are taught to be suspicious of people whose favourite song is *My Way*. They always turn out to be dictators or egomaniacs of one kind or another. So here's an Elizabethan version. It is by Sir Henry Wotton, who was once ambassador to Venice and made the famous crack that a diplomat is an honest man sent to lie abroad for his country.

For years I used to warble it at school on a Sunday evening – there is a beautiful tune – without really thinking about the words, until gradually I saw what terrific advice old Sir Henry was giving. It's about independence of mind and spirit and not giving a damn what people say. It's about the liberation that comes with trying to tell the truth exactly as you see it and it is to be recommended to anyone contemplating a career in politics, or journalism, or indeed as any other kind of human being.

The Character of a Happy Life
Sir Henry Wotton

How happy is he born and taught
That serveth not another's will;
Whose armour is his honest thought,
And simple truth his utmost skill!

Whose passions not his masters are;
Whose soul is still prepared for death,
Untied unto the world by care
Of public fame or private breath;

Who envies none that chance doth raise,
Nor vice; who never understood
How deepest wounds are given by praise;
Nor rules of state, but rules of good;

Who hath his life from rumours freed;
Whose conscience is his strong retreat;
Whose state can neither flatterers feed,
Nor ruin make oppressors great;

Who God doth late and early pray
More of His grace than gifts to lend;
And entertains the harmless day
With a religious book or friend;

This man is freed from servile bands
Of hope to rise or fear to fall:
Lord of himself, though not of lands,
And having nothing, yet hath all.

Boris Johnson has been mayor of London since May 2008. He was MP for Henley on Thames from 2001 to 2008 and held shadow government posts as vice chairman, shadow minister for the arts and shadow minister of higher education.

In a media career spanning 20 years he has been a columnist for *The Daily Telegraph*, editor of *The Spectator* from 1999 to 2005 and has also produced a TV series on Roman history, as well as several books. A passionate cyclist, he enjoys painting and playing tennis. He spends much of his time bringing up his four children with his wife Marina in north London.

Catherine Allen

"Those words gave me hope, strength and the determination to give myself and my life, back to me."

I'm Still Here
John Rzeznik

This song came out in 2002 and was in the Disney movie, *Treasure Planet*. At the time I first found it, I was still grieving for my mother who had passed away in 2005. I was in foster care when she died and her death was very unexpected.

I felt left out from life and that no-one knew who I really was. I was alone and completely numb in my own body and in the environment around me.

Because I was now an orphan, there was no-one there to show me and tell me what was going on, or to help guide me through my teenage years and into adulthood. I felt isolated and depressed because nobody knew what to do with me. I seemed like a guest or piece of furniture in someone else's home. I wanted to belong somewhere and not be a guest or a child who would be kicked out when troublesome or too old.

This song gave me the words to describe how I was feeling. I was only 15, but for the second time in my life I had so many different and powerful emotions. All I could do was shut down, which is what happened.

My GCSEs suffered badly. I only achieved one of my predicted grades – the rest were Ds, Es and Fs.

The song was able to give me one thing. It was the only thing that was given to me while I was in foster care that meant something. Three words – very small, ordinary words – which are "I'm still here". They gave me hope, strength and the determination to give myself and my life, back to me. I am the one who chooses the course of my life. I am not a piece of furniture that gets moved by others.

My parents are gone. I know that and I have to come to terms with it. But I shall carry on. I will give myself the things that most people take for granted such as a home, a job, a family. Even though I lost two of those long ago, I will make my own. I've already given myself a home, a job to support my home and I'm confident about my future.

This song will always be special to me whenever I hear it. I think back to when I heard it and how I felt then. But I also think how far I have come since then and also that the future has endless possibilities for me.

I'm Still Here
John Rzeznik

I am a question to the world
Not an answer to be heard
Or a moment that's held in your arms

And what do you think you'd ever say
I won't listen anyway
You don't know me
And I'll never be what you want me to be

And what do you think you'd understand
I'm a boy – No, I'm a man
You can't take me and throw me away
And how can you learn what's never shown
Yeah you stand here on your own
They don't know me
'Cause I'm not here

And I want a moment to be real
Wanna touch things I don't feel
Wanna hold on and feel I belong
And how can the world want me to change
They're the ones that stay the same
They don't know me
'Cause I'm not here

And you see the things they never see
All you wanted I could be
Now you know me and I'm not afraid
And I want to tell you who I am
Can you help me be a man
They can't break me
As long as I know who I am

And I want a moment to be real
Wanna touch things I don't feel
Wanna hold on and feel I belong
How can the world want me to change
They're the ones that stay the same
They can't see me
But I'm still here

They can't tell me who to be
'Cause I'm not what they see
Yeah the world is still sleepin'
While I keep on dreamin' for me
And their words are just whispers and lies
That I'll never believe

And I want a moment to be real
Wanna touch things I don't feel
Wanna hold on and feel I belong
And how can they say I'll never change
They're the ones that stay the same
I'm the one now
'Cause I'm still here

I'm the one
'Cause I'm still here
I'm still here
I'm still here
I'm still here.

Catherine Allen has been in and out of foster care since the age of 11. While in care she had three foster placements, two of which made her feel as if she was somebody's problem instead of a person. Before the age of 16, Catherine lost both parents and her feelings were all over the place.

Although her final foster placement was in many ways a more positive experience, she constantly felt uncertain about her future. However during this placement she learnt to let down the barriers and allowed herself to enjoy being a teenager.

Catherine was matched with a mentor through The Prince's Trust. Donna was around to support and encourage Catherine and as a result, she started to feel stable and secure in her life by getting her own home. When she was in care, she always felt she was a visitor in someone else's home so Catherine is happy to have a place to call her own.

Catherine is now in her first year at university studying Sports Management and feels this wouldn't have been possible without The Trust.

"I love the melody of this piece but it's the words that get me."

How Can I Keep From Singing?
Robert Wadsworth Lowry

In 2001, it was my first year of going solo and I was embarking on a brand new journey. It was a very exciting time for me, but anything new puts you out of your comfort zone. I think that when you are in this position, it's nice to have things that are comforting.

One of these things was the hymn, *How Can I Keep From Singing?*, which I found in an old book. I am always collecting them and have hundreds of genres. What I particularly look at are the guitar chords to see if I like the melody and also the words.

I love the melody of this piece but it is the words that get me: "No storm can shake my inmost calm. While to that refuge clinging. Since Christ is Lord of Heav'n and earth. How can I keep from singing?"

I performed this song in front of Bill Clinton at the Hay-on-Wye Literary Festival. It was my first public show and I thought it would be nice to sing him something that would resonate with his country's history as the song became popular during the American Civil War.

Cerys Matthews is a Welsh singer/songwriter, best known as the lead singer of rock band Catatonia, for her 1999 Christmas duet with Tom Jones and her 2007 appearance on *I'm a Celebrity...Get Me Out of Here!*

Born in Wales, Cerys moved to Nashville, Tennessee, in early summer 2002 where she started her solo career. Cerys has been involved with The Trust for about eight years and also became the vice president of the Welsh homelessness charity Shelter Cymru in 2008. She strongly believes that a person's most basic needs are to feel safe and secure in their own home.

How Can I Keep From Singing?

Robert Wadsworth Lowry

My life flows on in endless song;
Above earth's lamentation
I hear the sweet though far off hymn
That hails a new creation:
Through all the tumult and the strife
I hear the music ringing;
It finds an echo in my soul—
How can I keep from singing?

What though my joys and comforts die?
The Lord my Savior liveth;
What though the darkness gather round!
Songs in the night He giveth:
No storm can shake my inmost calm
While to that refuge clinging;
Since Christ is Lord of Heav'n and earth,
How can I keep from singing?

I lift mine eyes; the cloud grows thin;
I see the blue above it;
And day by day this pathway smoothes
Since first I learned to love it:
The peace of Christ makes fresh my heart,
A fountain ever springing:
All things are mine since I am His—
How can I keep from singing?

"I love this song and I always have."

Lawrence KS
Josh Ritter

I love this song and I always have. Josh Ritter is one of the few artists that I have never grown out of. I listen to all kinds of music and artists and can appreciate most sounds. But whereas I will be obsessed with an album for a couple of weeks and then never put it on again, I always come back to Josh.

The story behind this particular song goes as follows. My best friend, Ned and I had been lucky enough to be driving across the USA from Los Angeles to New York on motorbikes. It was the trip of a lifetime and no two people knew this better than us. A week or so into our trip and while we were making our way through Kansas, we had got a little lost and were studying a map trying to determine where we should head to for the night. We needed a place that was big enough to have a motel but also close enough for us to get there by nightfall.

We settled on a town about three hours away and got back on the road. I was listening to Josh Ritter on my iPod when we started seeing signs for our destination and it dawned on me that I was listening to a song about the town we were entering. It had been one of my favourites for a long time but us choosing to stop there was a complete coincidence. I pulled over to tell Ned and together we rode into Lawrence, Kansas, singing along to the song of the same name. It was a great feeling.

One of the lines in this song is "I've been from here to Lawrence, Kansas..." and now I actually have!

Lawrence KS
Josh Ritter

Dirt roads and dryland farming might be the death of me
But I can't leave this world behind
Debts are not like prison where there's hope of getting free
And I can't leave this world behind

I've been from here to Lawrence, Kansas
Trying to leave my state of mind
Trying to leave this awful sadness
But I can't leave this world behind

South of Delia there's a patch out back by the willow trees
And I can't leave this world behind
It's a fenced in piece of nothing where I hear voices on my knees
And I can't leave this world behind

Some prophecies are self-fulfilling
But I've had to work for all of mine
Better times will come to me, God willing
Cause I can't leave this world behind

This world must be frightening everybody's on the run
And I can't leave this world behind
And my house is a wooden one and its built on a wooden one
Seems I can't leave this world behind

Preacher says when the Master calls us
He's gonna give us wings to fly
But my wings are made of hay and corn husks
So I can't leave this world behind

Charlie Cox is an English actor, who having appeared in BBC Television's hit series *Judge John Deed*, decided to attend The Bristol Old Vic Theatre School. Since graduating, Charlie has starred in the leading role of Tristan Thorn in the 2007 movie *Stardust* along side Robert De Niro and Michelle Pfeiffer.

More recently he appeared in Harold Pinter's *The Lover* and *The Collection* in London's West End and has just finished filming *1939* for Writer/Director Stephen Poliakoff.

Charlie has been a Prince's Trust ambassador for over three years and presented an award at the Celebrate Success Awards UK final in 2008.

"Louis Armstrong became my hero and music my solace."

Hand Me Down My Silver Trumpet
Traditional

This is an old spiritual that I learned when I was four years old. Later that same year I had to go and live with my grandparents in the English countryside. I missed my mum, dad and sister so much I became a little reclusive and I would quietly go off and play on the piano in the parlour.

My grandad, Joe Brudenell, who had been a British Army cornet player, sensed I was musical. In his wisdom he gave me his silver cornet. This changed my life. When I returned to my parents I was taught to play by Mr Kempson. That cornet has been a treasured friend ever since and this simple song became prophetic. Louis Armstrong became my hero and music my solace.

Colin Salmon is one of Britain's most renowned actors, best known for his deep voice and role as Charles Robinson in the James Bond films, *Tomorrow Never Dies, The World is Not Enough* and *Die Another Day.*

He made his debut in 1992 as Sgt Robert Oswald in *Prime Suspect 2*. As well as appearing in other hit TV shows such as *Doctor Who* and *No 1 Ladies Detective Agency,* Colin has also starred in films *Resident Evil* and *Alien vs Predator.*

Colin, married to artist Fiona Hawthorne, was a guest call taker for the donation phone lines of The Prince's Trust 30th Birthday.

Hand Me Down My Silver Trumpet
Traditional

Well, I've never been to Heaven, but I've been told,
Hand me down my silver trumpet, Gabriel;
The gates are made of pearl and the streets are
made of gold,
Hand me down my silver trumpet, Lord.

Chorus
O hand me down, O hand me down,
O hand me down my silver trumpet, Gabriel
Send it down, hand it down,
Any ol' way, just get it down
Hand me down my silver trumpet Lord.

If religion were a thing that money could buy
Hand me down my silver trumpet, Gabriel;
The rich would live and the poor would die,
Hand me down my silver trumpet, Lord.

Well now, if you want a silver trumpet like mine,
Hand me down my silver trumpet, Gabriel:
You'd better learn to play it in plenty of time,
Hand me down my silver trumpet, Lord.

"The song has a clear resonance: it is a song about solitude, but more tellingly, loneliness."

Eleanor Rigby
The Beatles

When I was a child we used to spend summers in a beautiful big country house in Norfolk near Hunstanton. There was an attic that my brother and I would escape to and listen to music. They were summers full of the sounds of Madness (the first time round) and The Beatles (not the first time round). I was about ten.

In truth I might easily choose any one of their songs but as I sat daydreaming, looking out of the attic window, one song not so much inspired me as always haunted me and that song was *Eleanor Rigby*. As a young boy it was a collection of sounds and images only. But even then, at the age of ten, it was startling to hear a song open with a choral:

"Ah, look at all the lonely people"

Even more startling to hear that Eleanor, "Wears the face that she keeps in a jar by the door..."

Now of course as I sit daydreaming and staring out of windows, something I am almost always doing when sitting at my desk, the song has a clear resonance: it is a song about solitude, but more tellingly, loneliness. It is a beautiful song charged with a pulsing melancholy. As a ten year-old I would listen quite literally to the lines:

"All the lonely people, where do they all come from, All the lonely people, where do they all belong?"

Now when I listen to them I think more of how terrible loneliness is. That no one should be allowed to be lonely. That no one should be buried,

"...along with their name"

The most important thing we can do is to interact with one another. To embrace one another with all our faults. It comes with frustrations, sure. But nothing is as awful as loneliness.

Eleanor Rigby

Lennon/McCartney

Ah, look at all the lonely people
Ah, look at all the lonely people

Eleanor Rigby picks up the rice in the church where a wedding
has been
Lives in a dream
Waits at the window, wearing the face that she keeps in a jar by
the door
Who is it for?

All the lonely people
Where do they all come from?
All the lonely people
Where do they all belong?

Father Mckenzie writing the words of a sermon that no one will
hear
No one comes near.
Look at him working. Darning his socks in the night when there's
nobody there
What does he care?

All the lonely people
Where do they all come from?
All the lonely people
Where do they all belong?

Eleanor Rigby died in the church and was buried along with her
name
Nobody came
Father Mckenzie wiping the dirt from his hands as he walks from
the grave
No one was saved

All the lonely people
Where do they all come from?
All the lonely people
Where do they all belong?

British actor Damian Lewis studied at Guildhall School of Music and Drama. After graduating in 1993, Damian worked on the stage with the Royal Shakespeare Company. It was there he was spotted by director Steven Spielberg, who subsequently cast him as Richard Winters in the mini-series *Band of Brothers*, for which he was nominated for various awards including a Golden Globe.

In 2008, Damian starred as the main character in the popular US television series *Life*.

Damian is a trade justice ambassador for Christian Aid and is proud to be a Prince's Trust ambassador. He presented an award at the 2008 Celebrate Success Awards UK final.

> **Even today that voice and that melody take me instantly back to the atmosphere, excitement and adrenaline of that very special competition.**

Nessun Dorma
Luciano Pavarotti

I would readily admit that music is not my strongest point. I do have a slight musical claim to fame though – an involvement in the hit record, *World in Motion*. This was the official song for England in the 1990 Football World Cup, hosted by Italy. Along with the rest of the England Team, I performed on that recording, although you'll find it hard to spot my voice behind New Order and Keith Allen. The record made number one in the charts – not bad for someone who feels that he can't actually sing or play anything.

But there was another piece of music associated with that World Cup. It achieved far greater and more lasting fame than our record. It was adopted as the universal theme for the World Cup itself and was a complete departure from any of the football chants and songs that had gone before. Even today it remains a unique anthem for the sport. It was of course Puccini's *Nessun Dorma*, sung by the late amazing Italian tenor, Luciano Pavarotti.

In the World Cup itself we reached the semi-finals against West Germany. I was fortunate enough to score an equalising goal in the second half, which led us into a nail-biting penalty shoot-out. I've often wondered how many of us had *Nessun Dorma* playing in our heads in those nerve-wracking moments. Perhaps it would have helped if we had realised that the English translation of the final line is actually, "I will win! I will win!" Sadly however, we didn't and we were out – the only consolation being that the side who had beaten us went on to be the eventual champions.

Of all the vast international audiences who were glued to their televisions watching the football, there must have been many thousands who were inspired by that amazing piece of music. I was certainly one of them. Even today that voice and that melody take me instantly back to the atmosphere, excitement and adrenaline of that very special competition – and I know they always will.

Nessun Dorma
Giacomo Puccini

ITALIAN:

Nessun dorma! Nessun dorma!
Tu pure, o, Principessa,
nella tua fredda stanza,
guardi le stelle
che tremano d'amore
e di speranza.

Ma il mio mistero e chiuso in me,
il nome mio nessun saprá!
No, no, sulla tua bocca lo diró
quando la luce splenderá!

Ed il mio bacio sciogliera il silenzio
che ti fa mia!

(Il nome suo nessun saprá!...
e noi dovrem, ahimé, morir!)

Dilegua, o notte!
Tramontate, stelle!
Tramontate, stelle!
All'alba vinceró!
vinceró, vinceró!

ENGLISH:

No-one sleeps....no-one sleeps,
Even you, O Princess,
in your cold room,
Watch the stars
which tremble with love
and hope!

But my secret is locked within me,
no-one shall know my name!
No, no, I shall say it on your mouth
when the light breaks!

And my kiss will break the silence
that makes you mine!

(No-one shall know his name,
and we, alas, shall die!)

Vanish, o night!
Set, ye stars!
Set, ye stars!
At dawn I will win!
I will win, I will win!

During his playing career, Gary Lineker OBE was one of the best known and widely admired football players in the world. He made 80 appearances for England and was captain between 1990 and 1992. His goal total for his country places him second on the all-time list behind Bobby Charlton.

The end of his playing career in the mid-nineties was the beginning of what has become an illustrious involvement in television. He is now firmly established as the voice and face of BBC's flagship football programme *Match of the Day*. As a sportsman and celebrity he has been an inspiration to many thousands of young people. He is the holder of many awards including PFA Footballer of The Year, FIFA Fair Play Award and Golden Boot Top Scorer. In 1992 he received an OBE.

"The whole experience was magical."

Prélude à L'après-Midi d'un Faune
Debussy

Soon after the Second World War began, my school was evacuated and my entire family moved from central London to Bromley in Kent. It was a bit of an upheaval, but there was compensation in the very good music department at school. When I was 14, I was told that the BBC Symphony Orchestra and Sir Adrian Boult were coming to give us a concert in our own school hall. I had never heard a symphony orchestra before and to be honest, I thought it was going to be a boring time.

One of the pieces they played was Debussy's *Prélude à L'après-Midi d'un Faune.* When I listened to the orchestra playing it – while watching them scraping away on their bows on catgut, the woodwind piping away, some of them on double reeds – I couldn't really connect with what they were doing and with the wonderful sounds I was hearing. But listening to the music I really could see the little faun wandering through the forest down to the pool to take a sip of water. The whole experience was magical and this made me determined to find out more about music. I think this was the crucial point in my life when I realised that music was an inexplicable form of art and through that I suppose it led to my career making music with great musicians. It truly was an inspirational moment.

"...listening to the music I really could see the little faun wandering through the forest..."

Prélude à L'après-Midi d'un Faune

is a musical composition for orchestra by the composer Claude Debussy. Said by some to be one of his most famous works, it was inspired by the poem of the same name written by Stéphane Mallarmé. Although called a prelude, and of only ten minutes in duration, it is nevertheless a complete work in its own right.

Sir George Martin CBE is considered one of the greatest record producers of all time. As an arranger and composer he is sometimes referred to as the fifth Beatle, a title owed to his work as producer or co-producer of all The Beatles' original records as well as arranging and playing keyboards on many of the Beatles' tracks. In 1969 he established Air Studios in London and on the island of Montserrat. Although now retired from his post as chairman, he is still busy with many charities. In recognition of his services to the music industry and popular culture, he was appointed Knight Bachelor in 1996.

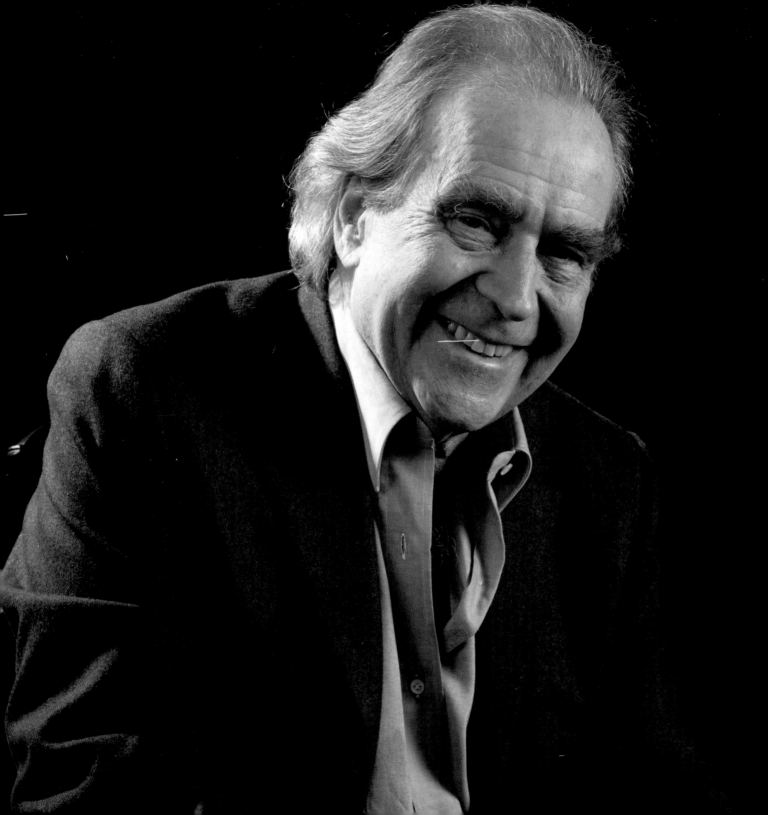

"As the song says, when you wish upon a star your dreams come true."

When You Wish Upon a Star
Ned Washington and Leigh Harline

In 1940, at the age of four, I was a huge Walt Disney fan and I have memories of waiting that year with bated breath for the film *Pinocchio* to be released. I remember my father took me to the New Regent Cinema, in Regent Street, but he was appalled to find that the seats were seven shillings and six pence, which he thought was too much for the family wallet so we didn't go in. I remember walking out into the street in tears. My father, seeing my disappointment, took pity and we went back, paid the 15 shillings and I had one of the most exciting afternoons of my life.

The following Christmas I begged my parents to give me a record of the soundtrack from the film. I was so excited on Christmas Eve I couldn't sleep and my parents, anxious to get to bed themselves, brought me back downstairs where I opened the precious present. We then played the record on the old-fashioned gramophone, which was as big as a sideboard. I gently lowered the needle onto the delicate acetate and the sound of *When You Wish Upon a Star* wafted through the house. During the following weeks I drew all the characters from the film – the fox, the cat, Stromboli and Pinocchio himself – and I feel they have all affected my work ever since. Fifty-four years later Disney asked me to be production designer on their animation feature, *Hercules* and I spent three years working with their animators in Hollywood. It was one of the best times of my life. I was treated like a star myself. It's the nearest thing I'll get to being Tom Cruise. As the song says, when you wish upon a star your dreams come true.

When You Wish Upon a Star

was written by Ned Washington and Leigh Harline.

It first appeared in the 1940
Walt Disney film *Pinocchio*,
sung by the character Jiminy Cricket.
Since then it has become a standard
popular song, being listed at number seven
in the American Film Institute's
100 Greatest Songs In Film History.

Gerald Scarfe CBE established himself as a satirical cartoonist, working for both *Punch* magazine and *Private Eye* during the early sixties. He has had many exhibitions worldwide and has designed the sets and costumes for plays, operas and musicals.

His film work includes designing and directing the animation for Pink Floyd's *The Wall* and Disney's *Hercules*. Gerald has written and directed many live action and documentary films and has published many books of his work.

His most recent books are *Gerald Scarfe: Drawing Blood and Monsters*. Gerald has been political cartoonist for *The Sunday Times* for 42 years and his work regularly appears in many periodicals.

Howard Schultz

"To me this song is a message of humanity and about being a part of something bigger than just ourselves."

One
U2, featuring Mary J Blige

I was recently reminded of something I once said, "One person can do only so much. But if he gathers a company of people around him who are committed to the same goals, if he galvanizes them and inspires them and taps into their inner drive, they can perform miracles together."

To me the song *One* is a message of humanity and about being a part of something bigger than just ourselves. I work for a big company, Starbucks, but it's the one-to-one human connections we form that matter the most – the connections with the farmers who grow our coffee, our partners who serve our customers and the neighbourhoods of which we are a part.

Bono and Mary J Blige's rendition of *One* is also a song of celebration. They sing with a soulful conviction that embraces diversity, the good times and the bad and the enduring hope for change. Through music, they ignite the power that we have as individuals and as a people.

We are all looking for inspiration. We live in a time when we all need to carry each other. I am inspired by this song and also by the true passion of the people I work with each day, their commitment to doing what's right and how they take care of one another and their communities. The call that we are in "one life, with each other" is a true anthem for today.

One was written and recorded by U2

as part of their 1991 album *Achtung Baby*.
Later released as a single, it has been acclaimed as
one of the band's greatest songs.
On the Rolling Stone list of "500 Greatest
Songs of All Time" it reached no 36.

At the time of going to print, we were unfortunately unable to obtain permission
to reproduce the lyric of the song in this book.

Howard Schultz, chairman, president and chief executive officer of Starbucks Coffee Company, had his first taste of Starbucks® coffee in 1981. Inspired by the experience, he joined Starbucks in 1982 as director of operations and marketing when Starbucks had just four stores.

In 1983, after a trip to Italy, Howard had a vision to bring the Italian coffeehouse tradition back to Seattle, creating a third place between work and home. That dream, along with the belief that social responsibility and profit can coexist, remain the foundation of Starbucks today, with more than 16,000 stores in neighbourhoods around the world.

Written in the Stars
Westlife

In 2007 a friend of mine sent me his version of a song which included a sample of *Written in the Stars* by Westlife.

At the time, Britain was going through major problems with gun and knife crime. In that year there were 18,489 gun crime offences, of which 59 were fatal and 22,157 knife crime offences, of which 322 were fatal.

A lot of these offences were being committed by and against people in my generation and I'd already spent time thinking about what my family would feel if anything like that happened to me. I decided to write lyrics for a track based on the message I would give my little sister if we, or anyone we knew, was ever a victim of this. When it was finished, I put this song up on my sites and within a year I'd had eight million plays.

I decided to make my own independent video for the song, featuring my little sister, to convey the message in the song and it was in the top three Channel U Charts for 26 weeks. People began to play the song at funerals and take it literally with what is going on in our streets. It was even quoted in *The Sun* newspaper as being "The Anthem for Broken Britain". I never ever could have imagined the impact the track would have.

Thanks to my video, I got called by a major record label who wanted to sign me up. I signed with them and my single went top five in the British national charts and has charted all over Europe and now in places like India, Russia, Sweden and the Czech Republic. The phenomenal success of this single allowed me to get an album deal with the same major label and I am now an established musician, DJ, producer and rapper.

When I heard *Written in the Stars*, I didn't even know it was by Westlife as that's not the usual music I listen to, or people from my genre of music listen to, but as soon as I heard it, I knew what I wanted to write about. I felt something that I really needed to put into words and what I wrote about was so relevant and personal, not only to me, but to thousands of other people, that it changed my life.

I'm only 21 but I feel like I've been lucky enough to have some sort of success and the fact that I have positively influenced people in my generation and others, makes me extremely proud of who I am and where I am in life. I am going to continue to write about true life situations in the most positive way that I can. If that influences at least one person, especially the younger generation, to be positive and work hard, then I will feel like I have done our society some good.

> **I found the chorus really moving so I decided to write about a subject that meant a lot to me – gun and knife crime.**

Written in the Stars
Jarl/Stenmarck/Carlsson

Stay with me
Don't fall asleep too soon
The angels can wait for a moment

Come real close
Forget the world outside
Tonight we're alone
It's finally you and I

It wasn't meant to feel like this
Not without you

Cos when I look at my life
How the pieces fall into place
It just wouldn't rhyme without you
When I see how my path
Seems to end up before your face
The state of my heart
The place where we are
Was written in the stars

Don't be afraid
I'll be right by your side
Through the laughter and pain
Together we're bound to fly

I wasn't meant to love like this
Not without you

Cos when I look at my life
How the pieces fall into place
It just wouldn't rhyme without you
When I see how my path
Seems to end up before your face
The state of my heart

The place where we are
Was written in the stars

I made a few mistakes, yeah
Like sometimes we do
Been through lot of heartache
But I made it back to you

Cos when I look at my life
How the pieces fall into place
It just wouldn't rhyme without you
And when I see how my path
Seems to end up before your face
The state of my heart
The place where we are
Was written in the stars

When I look at my life
How the pieces fall into place
It just wouldn't rhyme without you
When I see how my path
Seems to end up before your face
The state of my heart
The place where we are
Was written in the stars

The state of my heart
The place where we are
Was written in the stars

Ironik's professional career started at 13, when he began DJing regularly at the legendary TwiceasNice events. This led to shows on pirate radio and a flourishing DJ career. Next came production, a home studio and working with the cream of the UK underground – Roll Deep, Wiley and Chipmunk. It was while working with these artists that Ironik began writing, eventually becoming a consummate performer in his own right.

Fast forward to 2009 – the north London DJ, producer and MC has already taken the UK chart by storm last year with his debut single *Stay With Me* and acclaimed album *No Point in Wasting Tears*.

Jamie Turner

Iceland
Owen O'Mahony

Music is obviously pretty powerful and affects everyone, from the big names in this book to people like little ol' me. For some, it seems music has emotionally charged them to succeed. For others, music has changed their course of life in a very physical or literal way. For me it's definitely the latter.

Without delving too deeply, I guess my appreciation for music came from being, thankfully temporarily, deaf between the ages of 11 and 12. A few well-placed incisions and a long stretch in hospital (always with my mother by my side, for which I am endlessly grateful – thank you) meant that I regained my hearing. Well, most of it. This new-found appreciation for sound led to a passion for discovering as much music as possible and learning as many musical instruments as I could get my hands on.

It was in Cambridge when I found the music that literally changed my life. I discovered Hamfatter (as they were then called) while booking acts for the local Strawberry Fair festival. It was the only demo I received that made it past the first 30 seconds and the track *Iceland* stuck with me – so much so that I subsequently became their manager. A crazy idea and a stint on the BBC's *Dragon's Den*, some help from Peter Jones and now I find myself neck deep in the music industry doing what I love and working with the music that I love. A complete dream come true and it was all down to that one track.

Iceland gets played whenever I get completely daunted by the job at hand. I put it on and immediately remember why I do what I do. The world and its stresses disappear. The words detach me from reality and give me the escapism that I need to relax – an instant holiday – then I remember how grateful I am to actually be able to hear this music and especially how lucky I am to have a hand in sharing it. To me *Iceland* represents how much music can do and to quote another song that resonates with me, "You don't know what you got 'til it's gone." But if it comes back, boy do you fully appreciate it.

Along the way, The Prince's Trust has helped me with housing, education and mentoring, all of which had a huge part in getting me to where I am now. The Prince's Trust also, I guess uncharacteristically, funded an addiction I have – not to sex or drugs, but my unrehabilitational addiction to rock and roll.

Music's been good to me and I love that I am now part of the business that gets the music out to so many more people. Hearing all these inspirational stories of how music has positively affected people's lives makes me even more proud to be part of this industry. I hope that in doing what I do I can help encourage and inspire more people through music.

"The words detach me from reality and give me the escapism that I need to relax."

Iceland
Lyrics by Owen O'Mahony

Well we drive down south in the van with a bed in the back,
We do six hour shifts and a constant cup of coffee.
I really needed that day.
And it's fun to mess yourself up,
When you're cool and messed up already.
I really needed that day.
And oh, we really needed that day,
We really need it that way.
But oh, you're so desperately far away.

We stumbled down two flights of stairs,
I was burning up and I collapsed there in the foyer.
I didn't need it that day.
And they drove us out across the lava flows and the broken rocks,
And the unseen ice to the Northern Lights.
And I could hardly stand up.
But oh, you really needed that day,
I wouldn't stand in your way.
And oh, we're so desperately far away.

We hitched across tectonic plates to the Atlantic coast,
And looked down on the Gulf Stream.
And we booked a place on a tiny boat and as we sailed out the air got cold,
And our lives got dark.
But oh, we really needed that day to get away.
And oh, we're so desperately far away.

And we could find another way, move to a place where no-one knows us,
We could get away from all this and all the things that could destroy us.
We'd be happy every day and always, always looking gorgeous,
And we'd never have to deal with the people who ignored us.
All those years of pent up rage and all those years of taking orders,
Would be far behind us baby, we could get away from all this.

Jane Asher

"Hearing it still gives me a thrill – its simple but glorious tune and sweet words are a delight."

Poor Wand'ring One
Gilbert and Sullivan

When I was a little girl my father would often ask my brother, sister and myself to gather round the dining table and sing four-part harmony with him under his direction – sometimes hymns (in spite of us both being utterly unreligious, he had as strong a love for church music as I do), sometimes folk songs and sometimes extracts from a Gilbert and Sullivan opera. I realise now I was always a little grudging when these musical sessions came up – there was usually something 'better' I wanted to do, like watch television or meet my friends and I completely failed to appreciate the potential joy of singing accessible, fantastically enjoyable music as a family.

I look back on those times now, of course, with great nostalgia, not so much for the way they actually were – for, if I'm being realistic, I was probably pretty fed up for most of them, longing to escape and gossip with a school friend or slump in front of The Grove Family – but more for the unappreciated, gentle happiness of a time when the security of one's parents' love was assured and assumed and when, unknowingly, little seeds were constantly being sown in one's brain that would flower much, much later.

The Gilbert and Sullivan music was my favourite. I loved the songs and although there were many of the lyrics I didn't understand, I could sense that they were witty, charming and at times, cynical and extremely funny. As I had then a reasonably clear soprano voice and could sing in tune, my father persuaded me to sing Poor Wand'ring One solo and I remember experiencing that strange mixture of shyness and love of the spotlight that is typical of the actor. Being already a seasoned show–off, I quickly overcame the shyness and Poor Wandr'ing One became 'my' song – one that, I blush now to remember, I would happily sing at the drop of a hat to anyone willing to listen.

Hearing it still gives me a thrill – its simple but glorious tune and sweet words are a delight – and I'm quite sure that it was my early acquaintance with it and with the rest of the Gilbert and Sullivan canon, that led on to my love of music and to an adoration of opera: particularly those of Mozart, Verdi and Donizetti. It's very easy to dismiss Sullivan's music as being facile and schmaltzy, but it makes a fantastic introduction to classical music for the young. The seeds that hearing so much of it as a child sowed in me, have flowered into something that is an essential part of my life.

Poor Wand'ring One

Gilbert and Sullivan

MABEL:

Poor wand'ring one!

Though thou hast surely strayed,

Take heart of grace,

Thy steps retrace,

Poor wand'ring one!

Poor wand'ring one!

If such poor love as mine

Can help thee find

True peace of mind-

Why, take it, it is thine!

GIRLS:

Take heart, no danger low'rs;

Take any heart but ours!

MABEL:

Take heart, fair days will shine;

Take any heart – take mine!

GIRLS:

Take heart; no danger low'rs;

Take any heart – but ours!

MABEL:

Take heart, fair days will shine;

Take any heart – take mine!

Ah! Ah! Ah! Ah!

Poor wand'ring one!

Though thou hast surely strayed,

Take heart of grace,

Thy steps retrace,

ENSEMBLE

MABEL GIRLS:

Poor wand'ring one!

Poor wand'ring one!

Ah, ah! Ah, ah, ah!

Poor wandr'ing one!

Ah, ah! Ah, ah, ah!

Fair days will shine, Take heart,

Take heart, Take heart,

Take mine! Take any heart

Take heart! but ours!

Take heart!

Take heart!

Take mine! Take heart, no danger lowr's;

Take any heart but ours!

Ah, ah! Take heart, take heart,

Ah! Take any heart but ours,

Take heart! Take heart!.

Jane Asher is an actress, writer and businesswoman. She has been working professionally in film, theatre and radio since she was five years old and has written over a dozen non-fiction books and three novels. She has also developed a second career as a cake decorator and cake shop proprietor. Jane Asher Party Cakes has been located in Chelsea since 1990.

Jane is president of the National Autistic Society, of the Parkinson's Disease Society and of Arthritis Care, as well as holding many other roles in the voluntary sector. She has been a supporter of The Prince's Trust for many years.

"The whole world musically is in that song. It inspired me as a musician and a song writer."

For Once in My Life
Stevie Wonder

This is one of the first records I bought and although the total length of it is less than two and a half minutes long, everything is in the record.

Every element of the song is amazing! What the bass plays is fantastic. There's the drums, the two guitars, then there's the strings and they come in half way through along with the choir. There's a key change and Stevie Wonder sings it fantastically.

And then, on top of all of that, there's perhaps one of the greatest harmonica solos ever recorded. The whole thing inspired me and made me realise, if you can do that in two and a half minutes, if you take any longer, what're you doing exactly? The whole world musically is in that song. It inspired me as a musician and a song writer.

Also the fact that when I heard it when I was ten or 12 years old, I thought it was a fantastic piece and as I've gone back to it over the years it's become bigger. It's better than I thought in the first place and that's a very good measure of any piece of music that you like.

Some things you quite like and you come back to them a few years later and in fact they're not as important to you or you realise it was a fun thing but it's gone, like a loud jacket you had at the time. You come back to this song and you see something else, you notice another little detail, like looking at a fantastic painting.

It has every element that you could want. I listened to it just the other day and most of all I enjoy listening to my crackly original copy of it. It's not for nostalgic reasons, I don't think of music like that. Great music doesn't sound like it's from any particular time to me.

When you get something that's really good, the more you come back to it, the better it gets and the more you look into it, the less you realise you know about it.

For Once in My Life
Murden/Miller

For once in my life I have someone who needs me
Someone I've needed so long
For once, unafraid, I can go where life leads me
Somehow I know I'll be strong

For once I can touch what my heart used to dream of
Long before I knew
Oooh Someone warm like you
Would make my dream come true

For once in my life I won't let sorrow hurt me
Not like it hurt me before
For once, I have something I know won't desert me
I'm not alone anymore

For once, I can say, this is mine, you can't take it
As long as I know I have love, I can make it
For once in my life, I have someone who needs me

For once in my life I won't let sorrow hurt me
Not like it hurt me before
For once, I have something I know won't desert me
I'm not alone anymore

For once, I can say, this is mine, you can't take it
Long as I know I have love, I can make it
For once in my life, I have someone who needs me

Jools Holland OBE is a British pianist, bandleader and television presenter. His work has involved him with many of the biggest names in the music industry, such as Sting, Tom Jones and Bono.

At the age of eight, he could play the piano fluently by ear and by the time he reached his early teens he was proficient and confident enough to be appearing regularly in many of the pubs in South East London and the East End Docks. When Jools was 15, Squeeze was formed and *Up The Junction* and *Cool For Cats* made their success meteoric.

In 1987, Jools formed The Jools Holland Big Band – comprising himself and Gilson Lavis. This has gradually metamorphosed into the current 20-piece Rhythm & Blues Orchestra, which consists of pianist, organist, drummer, three female vocals, guitar, bass guitar, two tenor saxophones, two alto saxophones, baritone saxophone, three trumpets and four trombones.

Jools is one of The Prince's Trust longest serving ambassadors, having been involved for over 20 years.

Julien Hughes-John

"Music is a very empowering tool and has gotten me through some really bad times in my life. "

Rise and Fall
Craig David featuring Sting

From the very first time I heard this song, the words had an immediate effect on me. It was at a time when I was at my darkest and I had a lot of issues with self-belief. I continually beat myself up with a lot of self-criticism, which is always hard to deal with.

I was serving a seven year prison sentence at the very young age of only 22. I never imagined I would end up in that situation. I recall hearing this song on *Top of the Pops* and I was going through a real hard time thinking that there was never going to be any hope for me once I was released.

I actually managed to get hold of a copy on CD and within a day I knew all of the words and what really did it for me was the fact that I knew I was multi-talented and I could be successful, even though I'd been no angel and my life to some would have appeared to be over. Listening to this song gave me even more inspiration to be able to put my life in order and rise after my fall.

I am a changed man now, but still have an ongoing battle with my past. I will always use this song to motivate and inspire me – it always makes me emotional. I know with the right discipline and dedication anyone can make it.

Today, I am preparing for the 2010 Winter Olympics where I am representing my country in the Great Britain Bobsleigh Team. By chance, I was invited to the trials two months after my release and was really surprised when I got through them and was invited to attend my first season as part of the World Cup Team.

During the 2006/2007 season, I was part of the team that came fifth in the World Championships and fourth in the World Cup Finals. I became a British Champion in both the two-man and four-man events and was crowned Britain's "Fastest Brakeman" at the British Championships, all in my first year. Since being released from prison I have also managed to hold down a full-time job.

Music is a very empowering tool and has gotten me through some really bad times in my life. I now use this song to warm up to before a competition race and it gets me every time!

Many thanks to Craig David and Sting for releasing this great song and I hope it helps motivate and inspire other young people.

Rise and Fall

David/Sumner/Miller

Sometimes in life you feel the fight is over,
And it seems as though the writing's on the wall,
Superstar you finally made it,
But once your picture becomes tainted,
It's what they call,
The rise and fall

I always said that I was gonna make it,
Now it's plain for everyone to see,
But this game I'm in don't take no prisoners,
Just casualties,
I know that everything is gonna change,
Even the friends I knew before me go,
But this dream is the life I've been searching for,
Started believing that I was the greatest,
My life was never gonna be the same,
Cause with the money came a different status,
That's when things change,
Now I'm too concerned with all the things I own,
Blinded by all the pretty girls I see,
I'm beginning to lose my integrity

Sometimes in life you feel the fight is over,
And it seems as though the writing's on the wall,
Superstar you finally made it,
But once your picture becomes tainted,
It's what they call,
The rise and fall

I never used to be a troublemaker,
Now I don't even wanna please the fans,
No autographs,
No interviews,
No pictures,
And less demands,
Given advice that was clearly wrong,

The type that seems to make me feel so right,
But some things you may find can take over your life,
Burnt all my bridges now I've run out of places,
And there's nowhere left for me to turn,
Been caught in compromising situations,
I should have learnt,
From all those times I didn't walk away,
When I knew that it was best to go,
Is it too late to show you the shape of my heart,

Sometimes in life you feel the fight is over,
And it seems as though the writing's on the wall,
Superstar you finally made it,
But once your picture becomes tainted,
It's what they call,
The rise and fall

Now I know,
I made mistakes,
Think I don't care,
But you don't realise what this means to me,
So let me have,
Just one more chance,
I'm not the man I used to be,
Used to be
Sometimes in life you feel the fight is over,
And it seems as though the writing's on the wall,
Superstar you finally made it,
But once your picture becomes tainted,
It's what they call,
The rise and fall

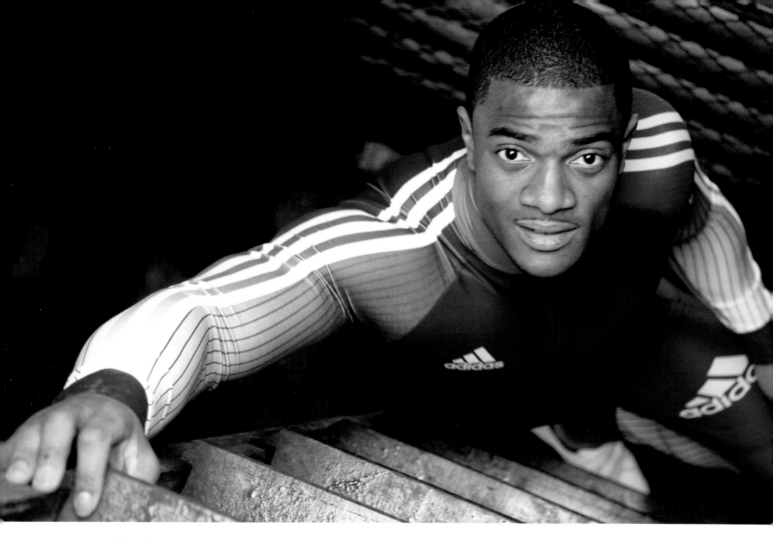

Julien Hughes-John had served four years of a seven year prison sentence when he was released in 2006.

A self-confessed fitness fanatic, Julien had been training in a local gym when he was spotted by a selector for the British National Bobsleigh Team. He was so impressed with Julien's fitness and physique that he asked him to try out with the National Team.

After attending a trial, Julien was invited to join the team. However due to lack of funding available at the time, Julien was advised he needed £4,000 worth of equipment. He approached The Trust who helped him apply for a Development Award and also look at alternative sources of funding. Through various Trust contacts, Julien raised the money he needed. In March 2007 he started training and in September 2007 was competing.

During all of his training and competing, Julien has managed to hold down a full-time job as a personal trainer and is looking at starting his own business.

" ...it is one of those numbers that I find truly moving and poignant to perform. "

In the Wee Small Hours of the Morning
Frank Sinatra

This is one of the greatest numbers that Sinatra ever recorded at Capitol Records. It is a moody, late-night kind of song, you'd expect to hear in a blues bar or jazz joint. The kind where smoke drifts through the single spotlight on the stage and a crowd leans in to hear the tale of a lost love. It's a dreamy and effective number and, as sung by Frank, a deeply moving interpretation.

I first heard it when I was about five, as my mother was a great fan of Sinatra and so I grew up in a home with these kind of great standards playing all the time. Listening to it now brings back so many memories of my first introduction to the great music and players of the past. I've also had the chance to sing it with a big band and it is one of those numbers that I find truly moving and poignant to perform. I say you couldn't do better than to put a log on the fire, stir up a warm drink, curl up with your favourite person and let Frank take you to another time, where clarity of voice and the rhythm of violins sweep away the winter night.

In the Wee Small Hours of the Morning

written by Bob Hilliard and David Mann,

is the title track of an album
by Frank Sinatra released in 1955
and often considered to be
the first 'concept album'.

The song summarises and reflects
the mood of the album as a whole,
namely lost love and late-night isolation.

For copyright reasons we are unfortunately unable to reproduce the lyric in this book

Kevin Spacey is an actor, director, screenwriter and producer. He began his career as a stage actor during the 1980s, before being cast in supporting roles in film and television. He gained critical acclaim in the early 1990s, culminating in his first Oscar for *The Usual Suspects* followed by a Best Actor Oscar for *American Beauty*.

Kevin has been artistic director of The Old Vic Theatre Company since 2003 and was recently honoured with a special Evening Standard Theatre Award for bringing new life to The Old Vic.

Kevin has been an ambassador of The Trust for many years and most recently presented an award at the UK final of the Celebrate Success Awards 2008.

"I thought it was awesome and so full of emotion and honesty."

Tears in Heaven
Eric Clapton

I was sitting in my room at my parents' house. About 17 years old. I loved music but I, like most people I guess, never really actually listened to all of the lyrics to the songs I liked at the time.

I was reading some books on computer programming and trying to make a website that sold logos for the Ericsson PH337 mobile phone.

Playing on my computer was a compilation CD which happened to have Eric Clapton's song, *Tears in Heaven* on it, a song I later learned he had written about his son who he had lost tragically.

I remember stopping my work and listening to the lyrics of the song repeatedly for the rest of the day. I thought it was awesome and so full of emotion and honesty. For some reason, even though it wasn't my first time of hearing the song, it just clicked.

I'm not sure if it's because of my religious background, but the question of your loved ones really knowing who you are when all the fun and games are over, resonated very strongly with my soul at that time.

I learnt the song and sang it to myself for ages.

A number of years later, when I was 24, my mother unfortunately passed away after battling with cancer for a few years. It was a hard time in my life and for the first time I found myself asking that same question and hoping that my faith and beliefs were true.

"Would you know my name, if I saw you in heaven. Would you feel the same, if I saw you in heaven."

I trust it will be the same – it has to be.

Music is a powerful thing and its beauty never ceases to amaze me; how one person's experiences, through voice and instrumentation, can give another person hope and strength to get through something in their own life.

Tears in Heaven will always be a song I hold close to my heart because of its honesty first. Somehow it gave me a little clarity when I was in between a rock and a hard place.

My aspiration is to write songs as moving as this.

Lemar is a singer/songwriter from London who rose to fame after appearing on Fame Academy in 2003. Despite being a runner-up, he has become its most successful graduate.

With four hit albums and six top ten UK singles under his belt, Lemar has helped redefine British pop music. Both the record industry and music fans acknowledged Lemar's contributions with two BRIT and three MOBO awards achieved over successive years.

Lemar takes time out to help people in a less privileged position than himself and is proud to be an ambassador for The Prince's Trust.

Tears in Heaven
Eric Clapton/Will Jennings

Would you know my name
If I saw you in heaven
Will it be the same
If I saw you in heaven
I must be strong and carry on
Cause I know I don't belong
Here in heaven

Would you hold my hand
If I saw you in heaven
Would you help me stand
If I saw you in heaven
I'll find my way, through night and day
Cause I know I just can't stay
Here in heaven

Time can bring you down
Time can bend your knee
Time can break your heart
Have you begging please
Begging please

Beyond the door
There's peace I'm sure.
And I know there'll be no more...
Tears in heaven

Would you know my name
If I saw you in heaven
Will it be the same
If I saw you in heaven
I must be strong and carry on
Cause I know I don't belong
Here in heaven

Cause I know I don't belong
Here in heaven

"It was a battle cry to the people who had let me down and a song of hope and freedom for me."

Something Inside (So Strong)
Labi Siffre

I can't remember the first time I heard Labi Siffre's *Something Inside (So Strong)* but it seems to be one of those songs that everyone knows and enjoys singing along to.

Songs have enough of an impact to remind me of certain periods in my life or to hold a significant memory for me, for both happy and sad times.

This particular song has always had a powerful and emotional impact on me no matter when or where I hear it. Like any other form of art, music is open to interpretation and this song spoke to me about my life.

Family breakdown and personal battles with anger and depression took me on a downward spiral into drinking and self-harm. I had no aspirations, no motivation, no sense of self-worth and certainly no hope…That is until I heard this song and really listened to the lyrics.

Labi Siffre's voice is full of emotion and the lyrics are full of empowerment and hope. It was telling me that no matter how lonely or beaten down I was, I could smash down the barriers and get through my personal troubles. It was a battle cry to the people who had let me down and a song of hope and freedom for me. It made me realise that I didn't have to be self-destructive or reliant on the wrong kind of people and that I could overcome my personal difficulties with strength and dignity.

When I look back at the girl who cried when listening to that song, it's like looking at a different person. My life is a different story now and I still can't quite believe how far removed I am from that lifestyle. My life now is full of positivity and personal achievement. I'm now using my personal experiences to inspire, help and motivate other troubled young people.

When I hear the song now, I have a private moment to reflect on what has been and what is now. It will always hold a special place in my heart.

I have cried many tears listening to this piece of music, but now I listen to it with a smile and the private thought – I did it.

Before joining The Prince's Trust personal development programme, Team, Lisa Daly was on a path of self-destruction after family problems left her traumatised and unable to cope. Unemployed and struggling with depression, drinking and self-harm, Lisa had lost any sense of hope and had given up on life.

At 24, Lisa was still eligible for Team, but knew it was a case of 'now or never'. She was not entirely sure how it would benefit her, but she knew she needed to make efforts to change her life. She took a leap of faith and through the programme she felt accepted and that she belonged to something for the first time in years.

Lisa excelled as a team player and it gave her a more positive outlook on life. She is now using her experiences to inspire other young people in her job as a Prince's Trust Team leader. Lisa has totally transformed her life through her sheer determination not to be beaten by the traumatic events of her past.

Something Inside (So Strong)
Words and music by Labi Siffre

The higher you build your barriers
The taller I become
The farther you take my rights away
The faster I will run
You can deny me
You can decide to turn your face away
No matter, cos there's…

Something inside so strong
I know that I can make it
Though you're doing me wrong, so wrong
You thought that my pride was gone
Oh no, there's something inside so strong
Oh oh oh oh oh oh something inside so strong

The more you refuse to hear my voice
The louder I will sing
You hide behind walls of Jericho
Your lies will come tumbling
Deny my place in time
You squander wealth that's mine
My light will shine so brightly
It will blind you
Because there's…

Something inside so strong
I know that I can make it
Though you're doing me wrong, so wrong
You thought that my pride was gone
Oh no, there's something inside so strong
Oh oh oh oh oh oh something inside so strong

Brothers and sisters
When they insist we're just not good enough
Well we know better
Just look 'em in the eyes and say
We're gonna do it anyway
We're gonna do it anyway

There's…

Something inside so strong
And I know that I can make it
Though you're doing me wrong, so wrong
You thought that my pride was gone
Oh no, there's something inside so strong
Oh oh oh oh oh oh something inside so strong

Brothers and sisters
When they insist we're just not good enough
Well we know better
Just look 'em in the eyes and say
We're gonna do it anyway
We're gonna do it anyway
We're gonna do it anyway
We're gonna do it anyway
Because there's

Something inside so strong
I know that I can make it
Though you're doing me wrong, so wrong
You thought that my pride was gone
Oh no, there's something inside so strong

There's something inside so strong
I know that I can make it
Though you're doing me wrong, so wrong
You thought that my pride was gone
Oh no, there's something inside so strong
Oh oh oh oh oh oh
Something inside so strong
Oh oh oh oh oh oh
Something inside so strong
Oh oh oh oh
Something inside so strong

Mark Ronson

"...there was something so effortless and almost accidental about the way it sounded..."

Fools Gold
The Stone Roses

I moved to New York when I was eight and my musical upbringing was very different. All my friends listened to hip hop from the age of 11 and we'd all be singing De La Soul songs on the school bus ride to sport games. It was all about A Tribe Called Quest, Run DMC, Public Enemy, Beastie Boys, late 80s early 90s and I loved it. I loved the rhythm tracks and growing up my dad loved funk and it spoke to me.

I would go back and forth to London once or twice a year to visit my dad and this was where I discovered Brit Pop. I remember going to a record shop in Notting Hill one time and seeing a nine minute version of *Fools Gold* by The Stone Roses.

I recall hearing it and it changed my entire musical perspective because it was a combination of New York hip hop and the British pop melody. This song combined both of those – it had that amazing sampled break-beat with this haunting, incredible melody delivered by Ian Brown.

It was the first time I'd ever heard anybody really combine those two things. Some of the bands like Happy Mondays and Primal Scream have made some great records sampling break-beats and combining them with more indie-ish melodies, but there was something so effortless and almost accidental about the way it sounded from The Stone Roses, the way they put the song together.

I think even my own record, *Version*, was my take on songs primarily from the modern British pop canon of modern music, those certain types of melodies that came from The Beatles, through The Kinks and down to The Smiths, to Radiohead and the Kaiser Chiefs. Taking songs like that and putting them with more classic hip hop and break-beat, influenced backing tracks and that took me back to where I'm from.

Fools Gold

Squire/Brown

The gold roads sure a long road
Winds on through the hills for fifteen days
The pack on my back is aching
The straps seem to cut me like a knife
The gold road's sure a long road
Winds on through the hills for fifteen days
The pack on my back is aching
The straps seem to cut me like a knife

I'm no clown I won't back down
I don't need you to tell me what's going down
Down down down down da down down down
Down down down down da down down down

I'm standing alone
I'm watching you all
I'm seeing you sinking
I'm standing alone
You're weighing the gold
I'm watching you sinking
Fools gold

These boots were made for walking
The Marquis de Sade don't wear no boots like these
Gold's just around the corner
Breakdowns coming up round the bend

Sometimes you have to try to get along dear
I know the truth and I know what you're thinking

Down down down down da down down down

I'm standing alone
I'm watching you all
I'm seeing you sinking
I'm standing alone
You're weighing the gold
I'm watching you sinking
Fools gold

Fools gold

I'm standing alone
I'm watching you all
I'm seeing you sinking
I'm standing alone
You're weighing the gold
I'm watching you sinking
Fools gold

Artist Mark Ronson is internationally renowned as one of the world's finest music producers and DJs. Since his early DJing days at the age of 17, Mark has released two of his own albums and co-founded a record label. He was named Best Male Artist at the 2008 BRIT Awards and won three Grammys in the same year.

He has produced tracks for various artists including Lilly Allen, Amy Winehouse and recently recorded a live version of *A View to a Kill* together with Duran Duran, released exclusively as a bonus track for the *War Child: Heroes* CD.

> ## "The lyrics are beautiful and poetic but it's slightly unclear as to what's going on."

Song to the Siren
Tim Buckley

First of all it's a beautiful song and it always makes me cry. The thing it makes me think of is my daughter and I remember hearing it first not long after she was born. There's a line it – "Swim to me, let me enfold you" – and it just makes me think of my daughter swimming to me, her being born and me being away from her.

It's also a very sad song. The lyrics are beautiful and poetic but it's slightly unclear as to what's going on. It's the siren call that people find hard to resist and it's about not being able to stop yourself doing something that's going to be bad for you, destructive for you. There's a kind of terrible beauty to the song which I love. Lyrically it's great, musically it's beautiful and I love all the different versions of it. There's a very good version by This Mortal Coil, probably the most well-known version. There are techno versions, trance versions, folk versions – all kinds of stuff. It's just a wonderful song.

The very first version I heard was by a Northern Irish Elvis Presley impersonator and that's my favourite version, sung in the style of Elvis Presley. I've used it many times when I'm filming and I need to cry in a scene. Sometimes it's very hard to come up with the tears so I plug in my iPod and listen to this and that tends to get me in the right place.

Song to the Siren
Tim Buckley/Larry Beckett

Long afloat on shipless oceans
I did all my best to smile
'Til your singing eyes and fingers
Drew me loving to your isle

And you sang sail to me, sail to me
Let me enfold you
Here I am, here I am
Waiting to hold you

Did I dream you dreamed about me?
Were you hare when I was fox?
Now my foolish boat is leaning
Broken lovelorn on your rocks

For you sing, touch me not
Touch me not, come back tomorrow
Oh my heart, oh my heart
Shies from the sorrow

I am as puzzled as the Oyster
I am as troubled as the tide
Should I stand amid the breakers?
Or should I lie with death, my bride?

Hear me sing swim to me
Swim to me, let me enfold you:
Here I am, here I am,
Waiting to hold you

Recognised as one of the most talented of the new generation of British actors, Michael Sheen OBE is equally accomplished on stage and screen.

Michael has become known for his portrayals of well-known public figures: Tony Blair in the films *The Deal* and *The Queen*; David Frost in both the stage production and the film version of *Frost/Nixon*; and most recently, football manager Brian Clough in *The Damned United*. He also received a BAFTA nomination and the 2006 Royal Television Society Best Actor Award for his heart-breaking portrayal of performer Kenneth Williams in the BBC's *Kenneth Williams: Fantabulosa!*

His forthcoming role as a Muslim extremist in edge-of-the-seat thriller *Unthinkable* sees him working with Samuel L Jackson and is just one of many exciting projects Michael's working on in 2009.

Michael recently attended The Prince's Trust Celebrate Success Awards 2009 UK final, where he presented an award.

Nathaniel 'Natty' Sobhee

"I find it the most inspiring album I have ever heard. It's full of raw emotion and passion..."

Chan Chan
Buena Vista Social Club

The Buena Vista Social Club was a members' club in Havana during the 1940s. Through its popular dances and music events it became a focal point for Cuban musicians of the era to come together and play.

I find the Buena Vista Social Club album the most inspiring album I have ever heard. The whole thing was recorded in just six days and contained 14 tracks. It's full of raw emotion and passion and delivers strength to musicians and singers of all ages. The fact that many of these artists never received the credit and respect that they deserved until they were in old age is possibly one of the greatest stories in music.

In the 1990s, nearly 50 years after the original club had closed, Cuban musician Juan de Marcos González and American guitarist Ry Cooder were inspired by the Buena Vista legend to make a recording. They used traditional musicians from the Caribbean island, including some of the original performers from the club, to produce Buena Vista Social Club.

The album was released in September 1997 and became an unexpected success story. With very little marketing it became a huge hit, essentially off the back of good 'word of mouth'. It became the album everyone was talking about and as a result picked up a far wider audience than was usual for a world music release.

In 1998 it won a Grammy award and was listed as one of "The 500 Greatest Albums of All Time" by Rolling Stone magazine in 2003. It also spawned the Oscar nominated documentary of the same name which was directed by Wim Wenders.

"The way *Chan Chan* opens is haunting. It takes you through a roller coaster of emotions...""

To me this album brings hope when it seems so far away. In the times we live in now, when violence, crime and negativity fill our newspapers and television screens, this album makes me smile and encourages me. It makes me think, I'm only 33 and I've still got 50 years plus on these guys to do what I need to do. I mean, they waited eight decades to change the world – unbelievable!

In particular I have chosen the track *Chan Chan* written by Francisco Repilado, a four chord song that was to become "the Buena Vista's calling card." The way *Chan Chan* opens is haunting. It takes you through a roller coaster of emotions, opening with guitars and then trumpets. It grips you before releasing you to the mercy of the vocals that then strike you down with realism. This song is romantic, elevating and powerful.

The musicianship and tightness of the band is overwhelming. It is one of those songs that makes your hairs stand on end. Whatever your mood, it exists to uplift it and by the time the song has finished your soul has been cleansed, your mind has cleared and you feel as if you are ready to face every challenge.

The balance between the musicians and the vocalists is perfect – the space, the energy, the respect for one another. I also think this song captures the power and wisdom of these musicians. They are old men and one lady who wear their experience so gracefully. It's the perfect illustration of skills reaching their maturity.

These musicians are grateful, respectful and understanding of one another and the bond between them is evident when they perform. It's a bond that brings them together, as one, on a record that changed the face of Cuban music and world music as a whole forever. An album that was overlooked by the industry at the time went on to sell over eight million units and is still selling today.

"The voices of these musicians allows the whole world to hear how powerful music can be."

The Buena Vista Social Club was a turning point in my life and gave me strength through difficult times. When this album came into my life I was still angry with the world, with the opportunities I had missed out on, with the constant battle to be heard. I was too angry to have belief in my visions, my thoughts and my abilities, as wrapped up as I was in dwelling on the past or thinking too much about the future. With age comes wisdom and I believe this was the album that taught me this and walked with me through the transitional period from boy to man.

The Buena Vista Social Club helped me learn to live in the moment, for the moment and this has brought me great strength. That's why to me this album, but in particular *Chan Chan*, has a massive place in my heart and will remain there through my life.

Buena Vista Social Club is in my stereo, my computer, my DVD player and in me. It reminds me of where I have been and where I do not want to return. It has been an education, an inspiration, a best friend and a soul mate.

It's a reference point, a target, it's my old relationships, my new ones, my thoughts and my weaknesses, my expressions, my sanctuary, my awakening and my strengths. It reminds me that life is precious and that you should respect one and all.

The voices of these musicians allows the whole world to hear how powerful music can be. No matter what age, race, faith, religion or gender, we can overcome obstacles that stand in our way with a strength that comes from unity. This album shows that through hard work, focus and dedication, no matter how old you are or what your background is, anything is possible and if you really believe, anything can become your reality. I hope those who are not familiar with the Buena Vista Social Club and *Chan Chan* in particular, will now go and search for it. Sadly many of the musicians have now passed over but they have left the perfect gift – songs performed with a touch of magic and energy that will live forever.

Simply, *Chan Chan* gives us all hope!

Chan Chan

Words and music by Francisco Repilado

SPANISH:

De Alto Cedro voy para Marcané
Luego a Cueto voy para Mayarí

El cariño que te tengo
Yo no lo puedo negar
Se me sale la babita
Yo no lo puedo evitar

Cuando Juanica y Chan Chan
En el mar cernían arena
Como sacudía el 'jibe'
A Chan Chan le daba pena

Limpia el camino de paja
Que yo me quiero sentar
En aquel tronco que veo
Yasí no puedo llegar

De Alto Cedro voy para Marcané
Luego a Cueto voy para Mayarí

ENGLISH:

I'm going from Alto Cedro to Marcané
Then from Cueto, I'm going to Mayarí

The love I have for you
I cannot deny
My mouth is watering
I just can't help myself

When Juanika and Chan Chan
Sifted sand together on the beach
How her bottom shook and
Chan Chan was aroused!

Clean the dry sugar cane leaves
from the path
So I can get to that trunk
I want to sit down

I'm going from Alto Cedro to Marcané
Then from Cueto, I'm going to Mayarí.

For years Natty has been running Defcon Records, one of the seminal UK based Hip Hop labels. Following the label's success, Natty was signed up by the Extreme TV channel, presenting *Streetball* and producing music for *The Gumball Rally* (Channel 4). Natty has also performed at some of the best-known venues in Europe, as well as at outdoor events such as Glastonbury Festival. Working for so many years in the music industry, Natty is well placed to understand the struggles involved with creating music and gaining recognition and his experience equips him to inspire and mentor young people in his role as a Prince's Trust ambassador.

"When I hear that haunting melody on the Hammond organ I immediately become transfixed."

A Whiter Shade of Pale
Procol Harum

This may surprise most people who are well aware of my complete and utter obsession with The Beatles, but when I sat down and really thought about my favourite song of all time, I think I even shocked myself by choosing the Procul Harum classic, *A Whiter Shade of Pale*. To this day I do not know what the lyrics are about, but when I hear that haunting melody on the Hammond organ I immediately become transfixed.

I remember about four or five years ago I was in my home studio with my producer, working up a list of songs that I wanted to record for an album of rock covers which we later titled *Uncovered*. *A Whiter Shade of Pale* was at the very top of my list, when I was made aware of the fact that a close musical associate of mine had just recorded the song for his new album. It would have been odd for me to record it then so I took my pen and put a big fat line through the title.

Oh well…I'm hoping to get around to recording the song one day for a movie soundtrack or maybe just for my own pleasure!

A Whiter Shade of Pale

Reid/Fisher

We skipped the light fandango
Turned cartwheels cross the floor
I was feeling kinda seasick
But the crowd called out for more
The room was humming harder
As the ceiling flew away
When we called out for another drink
The waiter brought a tray

And so it was that later
As the miller told his tale
That her face, at first just ghostly,
Turned a whiter shade of pale
She said, there is no reason
And the truth is plain to see.
But I wandered through my playing cards
And would not let her be
One of sixteen vestal virgins
Who were leaving for the coast
And although my eyes were open
They might have just as well I've been closed
She said, I'm home on shore leave,
Though in truth we were at sea
So I took her by the looking glass
And forced her to agree
Saying, you must be the mermaid
Who took Neptune for a ride.
But she smiled at me so sadly
That my anger straightway died

If music be the food of love
Then laughter is its queen
And likewise if behind is in front
Then dirt in truth is clean
My mouth by then like cardboard
Seemed to slip straight through my head
So we crash-dived straightway quickly
And attacked the ocean bed

Written by Keith Reid / Matthew Fisher; Gary Brooker, the original composer of
A Whiter Shade of Pale, declines to share this credit until a decision is made by the
House of Lords in 2009. Published by Onward Music Ltd

Ozzy Osbourne's career has spanned four decades. Ozzy is a pioneer in his genre of music. He has helped open the door for countless bands by giving them their big break, by taking them on tour or by taking them on Ozzfest, his all-day metal festival which is now in its thirteenth year.

He has always been an innovator. Ozzy leads and others follow. He was the first front man to leave a hugely successful band and have equal or greater success as a solo artist; he was the first to have his own hard rock/metal touring festival and he was the first to have a celebrity reality television programme. There's no doubt that Ozzy's impact will be felt for generations to come.

"Whenever I heard it on the radio, I wanted justice and I wanted it immediately."

Blowin' in the Wind
Bob Dylan

I was a Martin Luther King kid. He is far and away the person who influenced me the most. He taught my American generation not just the possibility but the necessity of civil rights and non-violent protest. To this day I remember the roster of our civil rights martyrs – people like James Chaney, Andrew Goodman and Michael Schwerner, Medgar Evers and Viola Liuzzo – and the four little girls blown up in an Alabama church. When I became an adult I was equally as motivated for gay and lesbian rights. I remember our martyrs in that cause too; people like Matthew Shepard, Jody Dobrowski and David Morley.

The song that captured my feelings better than any other was *Blowin' in the Wind* by Bob Dylan. I was 14 years old when the version by Peter, Paul and Mary went to number two in America in 1963.

Dylan wrote many classic protest songs, several dealing with prejudice against African-Americans. The poetry and passion of *Blowin' in the Wind* particularly moved, angered and inspired me. Whenever I heard it on the radio, I wanted justice and I wanted it immediately.

Every time I heard and every time I hear the lines "How many deaths will it take till he knows, that too many people have died" I was and am filled with fury. We had to act for civil rights in 1963 and we have to today. It is what we have to do in our time.

Blowin' in the Wind
Bob Dylan

How many roads must a man walk down
Before you call him a man?
Yes, 'n' how many seas must a white dove sail
Before she sleeps in the sand?

Yes, 'n' how many times must the cannon balls fly
Before they're forever banned?
The answer, my friend, is blowin' in the wind,
The answer is blowin' in the wind.

How many years can a mountain exist
Before it's washed to the sea?
Yes, 'n' how many years can some people exist
Before they're allowed to be free?

Yes, 'n' how many times can a man turn his head,
Pretending he just doesn't see?
The answer, my friend, is blowin' in the wind,
The answer is blowin' in the wind.

How many times must a man look up
Before he can see the sky?
Yes, 'n' how many ears must one man have
Before he can hear people cry?

Yes, 'n' how many deaths will it take till he knows
That too many people have died?
The answer, my friend, is blowin' in the wind,
The answer is blowin' in the wind.

Radio and television presenter Paul Gambaccini currently appears on Radio 2, Radio 4 and Classic FM. Born in New York, he has been a national broadcaster since 1973. He appeared on Radio 1 for 18 years.

In 1995, Paul was named Philanthropist of the Year by the National Charity Fundraisers for his work on behalf of the Terrence Higgins Trust. He has recently been made a Prince's Trust ambassador.

Paul won the Sony Gold Award for Career Achievement in 2007. In January and February 2009 he delivered a series of lectures at Oxford University as the News International visiting professor of broadcast media.

"I've always been inspired by this childhood ditty..."

Incy Wincy Spider

I've always loved spiders, always been inspired by this childhood ditty that is all about never giving up however bad the odds are against you. By sheer perseverance, trial and error, it's possible to attempt anything. Just like Incy Wincy Spider.

Incy Wincy Spider

Incy Wincy Spider went up the water spout.
Down came the rain and washed the spider out.
Out came the sun and dried up all the rain
And Incy Wincy Spider went up the spout again.

Born in Mbabane, Swaziland and educated at the University of Cape Town, Richard E Grant came to England in 1982 to work on the stage and in television.

Richard has played the starring role in many films including the cult classic *Withnail and I.* More recently, he wrote and directed the 2005 film *Wah-Wah*, which was loosely based on his own childhood experiences in Swaziland.

Richard has been a Prince's Trust ambassador for ten years and supports The Trust whenever his filming schedule allows. He attends a variety of events and presented an award at the UK final of the Celebrate Success Awards in 2008.

Sean Diddy Combs

"It made me feel like I could do anything."

It's Like That
Run DMC

For me it was young, it was strong, it was black, it was powerful. It was hip hop and it made me feel like I could do anything.

It's Like That

Lawrence Smith/Joseph Simmons/Darryl McDaniels

Unemployment at a record highs
People coming, people going, people born to die
Don't ask me, because I don't know why
But it's like that and that's the way it is

[DMC]
People in the world tryin to make ends meet
You try to ride car, train, bus, or feet
I said you got to work hard, you want to compete
It's like that and that's the way it is
Huh!

[Run and DMC alternate lines for the remainder of the song]
Money is the key to end all your woes
Your ups, your downs, your highs and your lows
Won't you tell me the last time that love bought you clothes?
It's like that and that's the way it is

Bills rise higher every day
We receive much lower pay
I'd rather stay young, go out and play
It's like that and that's the way it is
Huh!

Wars going on across the sea
Street soldiers killing the elderly
Whatever happened to unity?
It's like that and that's the way it is

Disillusion is the word
That's used by me when I'm not heard
I just go through life with my glasses blurred
It's like that and that's the way it is
Huh!

You can see a lot in this lifespan
Like a bum eating out of a garbage can
You noticed one time he was your man
It's like that (what?) and that's the way it is

You should have gone to school, you could've learned a trade
But you laid in the bed where the bums have laid

Now all the time you're crying that you're underpaid
It's like that (what?) and that's the way it is
Huh!

One thing I know is that life is short
So listen up homeboy, give this a thought
The next time someone's teaching why don't you get taught?
It's like that (what?) and that's the way it is

If you really think about it times aren't that bad
The one that flexes with successes will make you glad
Stop playing start praying, you won't be sad
It's like that (what?) and that's the way it is
Huh!

When you feel you fail sometimes it hurts
For a meaning in life is why you search
Take the bus or the train, drive to school or the church
It's like that and that's the way it is

Here's another point in life you should not miss
Do not be a fool who's prejudiced
Because we're all written down on the same list
It's like that (what?) and that's the way it is
Huh!

You know it's like that and that's the way it is
Because it's like that and that's the way it is
(Repeat these lines 'til fade)

Sean Combs is known by his stage names Puff Daddy, P Diddy and now Diddy. Recently declared "One of the Most Influential Businessmen in the World" by Time Magazine and CNN, Sean oversees one of the world's preeminent urban entertainment companies, encompassing a broad range of businesses including recording, music publishing, artist management, television and film production, recording facilities, apparel and restaurants.

His business interests, under the umbrella of Bad Boy Entertainment Worldwide, include Bad Boy Records, the clothing lines Sean John, Sean by Sean Combs, a movie production company and two restaurants. He has taken the roles of recording executive, performer, producer (of MTV's *Making the Band*), writer, arranger, clothing designer and Broadway actor.

Sharon Osbourne

> " **The hairs on the back of my arm go up every time I hear it.** "

Bohemian Rhapsody
Queen

I was 23 years old when *Bohemian Rhapsody* was released in 1975. I still remember when I heard it for the first time. I was in a business meeting at EMI Records in London when a promotions rep pulled me aside to play it for me. I can honestly say I had never heard anything quite like it and probably haven't since. It was like a mini-rock opera. The song tells a dramatic story of a young man who commits murder and can't come to terms with what he's done. Every aspect of the song is truly brilliant – from the lyrics, to the vocals, to the harmonies in the middle section to the thunderous rock riff at the end of the song. The hairs on the back of my arm go up every time I hear it. *Bohemian Rhapsody* is a true musical masterpiece that still sounds relevant nearly 35 years since it was first released.

What I love most about the song is that it takes me back to that magical time in music, the 70s. What makes this story even sweeter is that a couple of weeks after hearing the song for the first time, I got to meet Freddie Mercury, Brian May, Roger Taylor and John Deacon and from that moment I was Queen's biggest fan. I travelled the world every chance I could to see them perform. Brian May even inducted my husband into the UK Music Hall of Fame 2005 which was a true honour.

We lost Freddie in 1991, but he still lives and breathes every time I hear *Bohemian Rhapsody*.

Sharon Osbourne is a music manager and promoter, television personality and presenter. Married to Ozzy Osbourne, she came into public prominence after appearing in *The Osbournes*, a reality television show that followed her family's daily life.

She later became a judge on the talent shows *The X Factor* and *America's Got Talent*. Her autobiography, *Extreme*, has sold in excess of two million copies.

After the success of *The Osbournes* and *The X Factor*, hosting her own chat shows and securing advertising contracts, Sharon was ranked as the 25th richest woman in Britain on the 2009 Sunday Times Rich List.

Bohemian Rhapsody
Mercury

Is this the real life
Is this just fantasy
Caught in a landslide
No escape from reality
Open your eyes
Look up to the skies and see
I'm just a poor boy, (poor boy)
I need no sympathy
Because I'm easy come, easy go
A little high, little low
Anyway the wind blows, doesn't really matter to me, to me

Mama, just killed a man
Put a gun against his head
Pulled my trigger, now he's dead
Mama, life had just begun
But now I've gone and thrown it all away
Mama ooo
Didn't mean to make you cry
If I'm not back again this time tomorrow
Carry on, carry on as if nothing really matters

Too late, my time has come,
Sends shivers down my spine
Body's aching all the time,
Goodbye ev'rybody – I've got to go
Gotta leave you all behind and face the truth
Mama ooo (any way the wind blows)
I don't want to die,
I sometimes wish I'd never been born at all

I see a little silhouetto of a man
Scaramouche, Scaramouche will you do the fandango
Thunderbolt and lightning very very frightening me
(Galileo) Galileo (Galileo) Galileo
Galileo Figaro
Magnifico
But I'm just a poor boy and nobody loves me
He's just a poor boy from a poor family
Spare him his life from this monstrosity
Easy come easy go, will you let me go
Bismillah! No, we will not let you go (let him go)
Bismillah! We will not let you go, (let him go)
Bismillah! We will not let you go, (let me go)
Will not let you go, (let me go)
Will not let you go, (let me go)
No, no, no, no, no, no, no
Oh mama mia, mama mia, mama mia let me go
Beelzebub has a devil put aside for me, for me, for me

So you think you can stone me and spit in my eye
So you think you can love me and leave me to die
Oh baby, can't do this to me baby
Just gotta get out, just gotta get right outta here

Nothing really matters
Anyone can see
Nothing really matters, nothing really matters, to me.

Words and Music by Freddie Mercury, © 1975
Reproduced by permission of Queen Music Ltd., London W8 5SW.

"The music still transports me instantly back to him every time I hear it."

Songs Without Words
Mendelssohn

He was called Ernest Alexander Nicoll but Nico is how everyone knew my grandfather. He was a brilliant orthopaedic surgeon, much respected in his profession for his work with injured miners in Nottinghamshire, helping them get back on their feet and return to work. But he was also my grandpa, the man with a naughty twinkle in his eye, a great presence and a wonderful zest for life. He inspired me.

At the age of 80, he was touring the world giving lectures about Elgar and his music. He taught himself Italian from scratch. But best of all he played the piano and he played it beautifully. At weekends when my sister and I stayed with our grandparents in their millhouse near Mansfield – first as children, later as young adults – we'd wake up to the sound of the piano drifting up through the house from the sitting room below. Schubert, Schumann, Debussy – he'd mastered them all. But it's Mendelssohn's *Songs Without Words* (Lieder Ohne Worte in C minor) that still transports me instantly back to him every time I hear it.

Grandpa died in 1993 at the age of 92. I'd just started work at the BBC as a trainee reporter in Manchester at the time. He'd got cancer and was dealing with it in a very no-nonsense, matter-of-fact way. I was devastated but he didn't want to see that. The cancer took hold very quickly and soon he was in hospital in Chesterfield for tests, then an operation. I rang the ward one Friday night to ask when I could visit him that weekend. He was too ill to talk. So I told the nurses I'd drive across the Pennines to see him that Sunday.

The next evening, after a long reporting shift at the BBC, I collapsed into bed exhausted and fell asleep. A noise woke me suddenly – it sounded like an alarm though I couldn't work out where it was coming from. It made a flat, continuous sound, like a heart monitor after someone has died. I looked at the clock – 1:30am – and fell back to sleep. The next morning I woke up crying, unsure why. Within minutes the phone rang. It was my mother. Her voice was breaking. Grandpa had died in the middle of the night, at 1:30am she said. I ran a bath and lay there, in tears, listening to one of the many tapes he'd made for me over the years. He was playing Mendelssohn's *Songs Without Words* – I'm listening to it now as I write this. The music, his voice on the tapes – it brings him straight back to me. There are some people who really make an impression on your life. He was very definitely one of them. I miss him hugely but I still have him with me when I hear his music.

Sophie Raworth has presented the BBC's *One O'Clock News* since June 2006.

She joined the BBC's regional trainee scheme in 1992 and went on to become a reporter for Greater Manchester Radio. In April 1994, Sophie moved to Brussels to become Europe reporter for the regions and in 1995 she returned to Leeds to *BBC Look North* and it was here that she first presented the news.

In 1997 Sophie joined *BBC Breakfast News*, co-presenting the programme four days a week.

Prior to joining the *One O'Clock News* Sophie was co-presenter of the *Six O'Clock News*, which she presented with George Alagiah from January 2003. She had previously presented *BBC Breakfast* alongside Jeremy Bowen from its launch in October 2000.

Sophie has been a Prince's Trust ambassador for more than ten years.

"I don't think you can listen to this song without feeling inspired, it could save anybody."

Don't Give Up
Peter Gabriel and Kate Bush

Gary

I don't think you can listen to this song without feeling inspired, it could save anybody. The lyrics are so inspirational.

Specifically, I was having a very low moment in the 1990s and this song came on the radio. There have only been a very few times when I've had to pull the car over to listen to a song – this was one of them.

The verses are very detailed and I love the contrast when Kate comes on and sings "don't give up because you have us" – it goes to the point. It's just a very well crafted beautiful song… it's just such a shame I didn't write it!

Jason

It's weird as Gary mentioned it years ago, not long after I got to know the guys.

My twin brother bought it on 12" vinyl and we used to play it all the time. It's one of those songs from our era where the music is a ballad – but not a smulchy ballad – that got our generation's ear.

Some of the lyrics really stand out for me – "rest your head you worry too much". We have heard all those lyrics before, but it's the way they sing them – it's Peter Gabriel and Kate Bush singing and the emotion makes it really believable. Perhaps in another context it wouldn't.

Howard

It was a majority decision and I got out voted. I would have chosen *Someone Saved My Life Tonight* by Elton John. Saying that, I really like the song and can see why it inspired Gary. If you're going through a low point in your life it's a beautiful song to sing.

Mark

I just really like this track and I love Kate Bush. It's such an inspirational song. A real performance – very honest and true, you believe every word they're singing.

Don't Give Up

Peter Gabriel

In this proud land we grew up strong
We were wanted all along
I was taught to fight, taught to win
I never thought I could fail

No fight left or so it seems
I am a man whose dreams have all deserted
I've changed my face, I've changed my name
But no-one wants you when you lose

Don't give up   'cause you have friends
Don't give up   you're not beaten yet
Don't give up   I know you can make it good

Though I saw it all around
Never thought that I could be affected
Thought that we'd be last to go
It is so strange the way things turn
Drove the night toward my home
The place that I was born, on the lakeside
As daylight broke, I saw the earth
The trees had burned down to the ground

Don't give up   you still have us
Don't give up   we don't need much of anything
Don't give up   'cause somewhere there's a place where
we belong

Rest your head
You worry too much
It's going to be alright
When times get rough
You can fall back on us
Don't give up
Please don't give up

Got to walk out of here
I can't take anymore
Going to stand on that bridge
Keep my eyes down below

Whatever may come
and whatever may go
That river's flowing
That river's flowing

Moved on to another town
Tried hard to settle down
For every job, so many men
So many men no-one needs

Don't give up   'cause you have friends
Don't give up   you're not the only one
Don't give up   no reason to be ashamed
Don't give up   you still have us
Don't give up now   we're proud of who you are
Don't give up   you know it's never been easy
Don't give up   'cause I believe there's a place
There's a place
Where we belong

Don't give up
Don't give up
Don't give up

Written by: Peter Gabriel
Published by Real World Music Ltd. Courtesy of petergabriel.com
© 1986 Peter Gabriel Ltd. Reprinted by permission (RWM200804-5) .
International copyright secured.

It was, incontestably, the pop story to end all pop stories, the unlikely triumph to beat all unlikely triumphs. Gary Barlow, Howard Donald, Jason Orange and Mark Owen, or Take That as they're collectively known, initially had success in the early to mid 1990's before splitting in 1996. However following a reunion tour in 2006, the group recorded their first studio album in over ten years.

Since the release of a second post-reunion studio album, *The Circus*, in December 2008 it has sold over 1.9 million copies in the UK alone. Their forthcoming summer stadium tour became the fastest selling tour in UK history with an incredible 600,000 tickets being sold in under four hours.

The group has supported a number of causes in the past including Comic Relief and the fight against poverty and homelessness.

"I loved the torture of it and the idea of being haunted by love."

Lilac Wine
Jeff Buckley

It's supremely difficult to single out one song as being particularly inspirational in my life, because there are so many songs and artists that have had a profound influence on my thinking, my emotional state and even my actions; I am very easy to lead astray via music. There is nothing as powerful as a song to invoke memories of a specific event and take one back to whatever was truly experienced at the time – for me, music can be a diluted form of time travel.

I have a very intense memory of hearing Jeff Buckley's *Lilac Wine* for the first time and whenever I subsequently listen to it, it takes me right back to that first occasion and reminds me of the tumultuous thoughts that plagued me during that short period of my life.

It was a period of change; I had just left school, I was working on my first film and had begun to be invited out to dinner in my own right. I was at one such dinner-party, feeling rather nervous and horribly unsophisticated next to my companions, when the nice man sitting next to me said, "Do you know Jeff Buckley?" I shook my head miserably, it being one more thing I had to admit to not knowing about. "I think you would like him," he said and asked that *Lilac Wine* be played. Our host had an extensive music collection and had been playing what I can only describe as 'very cool' music all evening.

As soon as it began to play I felt some transition within me. There was something settling in the melancholy of the man's voice. I wouldn't say it is my favourite song (hopefully I would choose something slightly more upbeat) but it certainly spoke to me that evening, probably because I could identify with the feeling of being out of one's depth. It's a very sad song, in a wonderful way, and I loved the torture of it and the idea of being haunted by love. I also found it vaguely exciting, as it was the perfect theme tune to my new bohemian existence, as I saw it. It made me feel quite grown-up.

I was given the *Grace* album cover to inspect and I noted how handsome Jeff Buckley was. They told me the story of his death – how he had wandered into the Mississippi River with his boots on, singing *Whole Lotta Love* and I had trouble holding back tears, as we listened to him lamenting in the background. I left the dinner feeling like I had discovered some marvellous secret and that I had aged 20 years in one night. I was heavy with the burden of the lyrics. I understood the idea of being unready for love – it was a time in my life when I felt very 'unready'.

Lilac Wine
James H Shelton

I lost myself on a cool damp night
I gave myself in that misty light
Was hypnotized by a strange delight
Under a lilac tree
I made wine from the lilac tree
Put my heart in its recipe
It makes me see what I want to see
and be what I want to be
When I think more than I want to think
I do things I never should do
I drink much more than I ought to drink
Because it brings me back you...

Lilac wine is sweet and heady, like my love
Lilac wine, I feel unsteady, like my love
Listen to me... I cannot see clearly
Isn't that she coming to me nearly here?
Lilac wine is sweet and heady, where's my love?
Lilac wine, I feel unsteady, where's my love?
Listen to me, why is everything so hazy?
Isn't that she, or am I just going crazy, dear?
Lilac Wine, I feel unready for my love,
feel unready for my love.

Words and music by James H Shelton
© 1949 (renewed) Chappell & Co. Inc. (ASCAP)

Talulah Riley was educated at Haberdashers' Aske's School for Girls. She attended Saturday classes at Sylvia Young's Theatre School and wanted to be an actress from a very young age.

She left school at 18 to film *Pride and Prejudice* for Working Title. She played Nellie in Adrian Noble's West End version of *Summer and Smoke* and has acted with Kevin Spacey in The *Philadelphia Story* at The Old Vic.

Talulah has worked on two further feature films, *St Trinian's* for Ealing Studios and Richard Curtis' *The Boat That Rocked*, as well as several television productions, including *Dr Who*. She loves dogs and lives in Los Angeles, California.

Talulah presented an award at the UK final of the Celebrate Success Awards in 2008.

Tony Blair

"The peace and serenity of it was a source of comfort."

Ave Maria
Renée Fleming

This is my favourite version of a beautiful song. The song itself is extraordinary, full of poignant emotion, building to a dramatic climax. She sings it magnificently. It matters to me because at a time when a close friend was dying, I used to play it and the peace and serenity of it was a source of comfort. Usually, I am – even after all these years – in thrall to rock and roll. This is an exception. But then it is an exceptional piece of music.

Ave Maria

C F Gournod

Ave Maria
Gratia plena
Maria, gratia plena
Maria, gratia plena
Ave, ave dominus
Dominus tecum
Benedicta tu in mulieribus
Et benedictus
Et benedictus fructus ventris
Ventris tuae, Jesus.
Ave Maria

Ave Maria
Mater Dei
Ora pro nobis peccatoribus
Ora pro nobis
Ora, ora pro nobis peccatoribus
Nunc et in hora mortis
Et in hora mortis nostrae
Et in hora mortis nostrae
Et in hora mortis nostrae
Ave Maria

Tony Blair, prime minister between 1997 and 2007, is now working in the Middle East, helping the Palestinians to prepare for statehood as part of the international community's effort to secure peace.

He has launched the Tony Blair Faith Foundation to promote respect and understanding between the major religions and to make the case for faith as a force for good in the modern world.

Having been the first major head of government to bring climate change to the top of the international political agenda at the Gleneagles G8 summit in 2005, Tony is now leading the Breaking the Climate Deadlock Initiative, through which he is working with world leaders to bring consensus on a new and comprehensive international climate policy framework.

"Even though I love it, I can't really figure out who is playing what on the record."

Like a Rolling Stone
Bob Dylan

I have many favourite songs. High on the list is *Like a Rolling Stone* by Bob Dylan. This record has always had a fascination for me because, even though I love it, I can't really figure out who is playing what on the record. I know there's a piano and a Hammond organ but I can't make out what they're playing and this is after spending the past 30 years in a recording studio.

Like a Rolling Stone
Bob Dylan

Once upon a time you dressed so fine
You threw the bums a dime in your prime, didn't you?
People'd call, say, "Beware doll, you're bound to fall"
You thought they were all kiddin' you
You used to laugh about
Everybody that was hangin' out
Now you don't talk so loud
Now you don't seem so proud
About having to be scrounging for your next meal.

How does it feel
How does it feel
To be without a home
Like a complete unknown
Like a rolling stone?

You've gone to the finest school all right, Miss Lonely
But you know you only used to get juiced in it
And nobody has ever taught you how to live on the street
And now you find out you're gonna have to get used to it
You said you'd never compromise
With the mystery tramp, but know you realize
He's not selling any alibis
As you stare into the vacuum of his eyes
And say do you want to make a deal?

How does it feel
How does it feel
To be on your own
With no direction home
Like a complete unknown
Like a rolling stone?
You never turned around to see the frowns on the jugglers and the clowns
When they all come down and did tricks for you
You never understood that it ain't no good
You shouldn't let other people get your kicks for you
You used to ride on the chrome horse with your diplomat
Who carried on his shoulder a Siamese cat
Ain't it hard when you discover that
He really wasn't where it's at
After he took from you everything he could steal.

How does it feel
How does it feel
To be on your own
With no direction home
Like a complete unknown
Like a rolling stone?

Princess on the steeple and all the pretty people
They're drinkin', thinkin' that they got it made
Exchanging all precious gifts
But you'd better take your diamond ring, you'd better pawn it babe
You used to be so amused
At Napoleon in rags and the language that he used
Go to him now, he calls you, you can't refuse
When you got nothing, you got nothing to lose
You're invisible now, you got no secrets to conceal.

How does it feel
How does it feel
To be on your own
With no direction home
Like a complete unknown
Like a rolling stone?

Trevor Horn, an English pop music record producer, songwriter and musician, has produced commercially successful songs and albums for numerous British and international artists.

With two Grammy Awards, three Brits and five Ivor Novelloes, Trevor has also built up a business empire comprising recording studios on both sides of the Atlantic and successful record and publishing companies.

To this day Trevor is still very much at the forefront of music production and most recently he has been working with one of last year's breakthrough success stories David Jordan, Simon Cowell's classical/pop quartet Escala, the latest signing to trend setting XL Records, Kid Harpoon as well as John Legend.

Trevor continues to take on a relatively heavy workload owing to his passion for music, something that has driven him for over 30 years as a frontline producer and continues to do so. He also supports several charities that are very close to his heart, including The Prince's Trust.

"This song is about oppression and faith. Overall, it is a call for unity."

One Love
Bob Marley

It is not only this song that has been a huge inspiration in my life but it's also the man who created it. I have Jamaican roots and Bob Marley is a national hero, in life and in death. He has done more for Jamaica in terms of challenging violence and increasing tourism than most of the country's politicians.

To me, Bob Marley's music is about day-to-day experiences as he knew them, including love, political repression and gangland warfare – an issue I can relate to. Growing up, I was involved in one of New York's most prolific gangs. My brother lost his life to that nonsense.

After my brother died, I wanted to turn things around and eventually I went onto modelling and acting. I got my big break when I appeared in the Fall 1994 Polo Sport campaign. That landed me an exclusive multi-year contract with Ralph Lauren. Since then I have worked with a number of inspirational and influential people, including Ben Stiller, 50 Cent, Britney Spears and Toni Braxton.

For me, the song *One Love* is about oppression and faith. Overall, it is a call for unity. This song has been relevant throughout my life. I was born to a Chinese/Jamaican father and a Panamanian/Jamaican mother and not so long ago I saw a large part of America unite to bring in the first black president.

As a father, this is definitely one of the songs I would urge my son to listen to. It deals with rising above people who have bad intentions for you and it also highlights the importance of respecting mankind.

I truly believe that Bob Marley is an inspiration to men and women from all races across the world. His music is uplifting and gives people hope for the future.

Tyson Beckford's modelling career exploded when he appeared in the Fall 1994 Polo Sport campaign. He landed an exclusive multi-year contract with Ralph Lauren and served as the spokesmodel for Polo Sport and Fragrances.

Tyson has appeared on magazine covers worldwide. His film credits include *Into the Blue*, *Zoolander* and *Biker Boyz*. He has also starred in music videos including 50 Cent's chart topping *21 Questions* and the Grammy Award-winning song *Toxic* by Britney Spears.

In his free time, Tyson is an active ambassador for The Prince's Trust. He is also busy developing his motor sports interests, which has led him to become a licensed driving member of SuperTuners and host of his own auto show.

One Love

Words and music by Bob Marley

One Love! One Heart!
Let's get together and feel all right.
Hear the children cryin' (One Love!);
Hear the children cryin' (One Heart!),
Sayin': give thanks and praise to the Lord and I will feel all right;
Sayin': let's get together and feel all right. Wo wo-wo wo-wo!

Let them all pass all their dirty remarks (One Love!);
There is one question I'd really love to ask (One Heart!):
Is there a place for the hopeless sinner,
Who has hurt all mankind just to save his own beliefs?

One Love! What about the one heart? One Heart!
What about – ? Let's get together and feel all right
As it was in the beginning (One Love!);
So shall it be in the end (One Heart!),
All right!
Give thanks and praise to the Lord and I will feel all right;
Let's get together and feel all right.
One more thing!

Let's get together to fight this Holy Armagiddyon (One Love!),
So when the Man comes there will be no, no doom (One Song!).
Have pity on those whose chances grows t'inner;
There ain't no hiding place from the Father of Creation.

Sayin': One Love! What about the One Heart? (One Heart!)
What about the – ? Let's get together and feel all right.
I'm pleadin' to mankind! (One Love!);
Oh, Lord! (One Heart) Wo-ooh!

Give thanks and praise to the Lord and I will feel all right;
Let's get together and feel all right.
Give thanks and praise to the Lord and I will feel all right;
Let's get together and feel all right.

Acknowledgements

The Prince's Trust Team

Kristian Hayter, Inspired* by music Project Manager

Mike Cobb, Head of Music Publishing

Naomi Edler, Head of Fundraising

Annabel Kirk, PR Manager

Laura Garbas, Marketing Manager

Annie Lycett, Head of ambassadors

Kimberley Perkins, Events and ambassadors Coordinator

Amie Hoyland, Head of Corporate Partnerships

Bernie Critchley, Events Executive

Paul Brown, Director of Marketing and Communications

Edward Percival, Head of e-Communications and Marketing

Dee Macdonald, Marketing Development Manager

Shoehorn Media Team

Simon Rix, Publishing Director

Eileen McLaughlin, Research Director

Faisal Sohail, Design, Layout and Retouching

Alex Belsher, Head of In-house Design

Alex Cornes, Design and Photographer's Assistant

Paul Simpson, PR Strategy

Starbucks Team

Jimmy Curtis

Luis Moreno

Darcy Willson-Rymer

Brian Waring

Amanda Royston

Sarah Dunne

Howard Schultz

Inspired* by music would have been impossible without:

Dawn McDaniel

Ondine

Maggie Hunt

Nicola Chapman

Emma Willis

The Prince's Trust would also like to thank the following:

Amy Grabow

Andrew Maurice

Angus Fulton

Ann Marie Bennett

Barry Navidi

Callie Gladman

Capricorn Clark

Cat Walker

Clear Channel Outdoor

Charlie Cobb

Chris Neil

Diana Murray

Ed Filugelli

Frances Mayhew

Frank Stork

Gaby Schuetz

Gilly Poole

Group Partners

Guto Harri

Guy Moot

Hans Meier

Ivan Chandler

Jason Eason

Jenny Gosling

Kara Darling

Kevin Abramowicz

Kew Bridge Steam Museum

Leah Webb

Maite Foriasky

Mark Beaven

Matthew Doyle

Music Sales (musicroom.com)

Peter Safran

Pierre Condou

Rob Bozas

Rory Carnegie

Rosie Mayhew

Royal Geographical Society

Sean Francis

Soho House New York

Sophie Raworth

Terry Whittaker

The Old Vic

The Paramount Club

The Setai Hotel Miami

The Suite

Wilton's Music Hall

The Prince's Trust would especially like to thank the publishers, composers and rights' owners who have most generously consented to the reproduction of lyrics.

shoehorn